BEGONIAS

BEGONIAS

The Complete Guide

Eric Catterall

The Crowood Press

First published in 1991 by
The Crowood Press Ltd
Ramsbury, Marlborough
Wiltshire SN8 2HR

British Library Cataloguing in Publication Data

Catterall, Eric
Begonias.
1. Plants
I. Title
635.93346

ISBN 1 85223 182 3

Typeset by Hope Services (Abingdon) Ltd
Printed in Great Britain by
Redwood Press Ltd, Melksham, Wilts

CONTENTS

ACKNOWLEDGEMENTS

In the pursuit of any hobby a considerable part of any progress made can be attributed to the advice offered by colleagues and friends. I would like to acknowledge, with gratitude, all those unnamed individuals who have, without hesitation, corrected my many shortcomings in the field of begonia cultivation. However, any errors in this book are my responsibility.

My affection for begonias began with the man to whom I shall be ever grateful, the late Secretary of the National Begonia Society, Fred Martin. And finally I owe my special thanks to my son Richard, whose patience was normally infinite, if occasionally a little thin. Without his help I am sure that this project could not have been completed.

INTRODUCTION

During the past eight or nine decades a number of books have been written on the subject of begonias, their history, development and cultivation. Of these texts perhaps half have clearly concentrated on the subject of Tuberous begonias, almost to the exclusion of any other examples of the genus, whilst the remainder have dealt with all begonias with the exception of Tuberous types. Books attempting to cover the practical cultivation of a wide range of begonia types are not thick on the ground, and in any case all but three or four have been out of print for many years.

As a fairly broad generalization books which dealt with Tuberous begonias have been written by European authors, whilst those covering the other types have tended to be the work of American and Japanese authors. This is not surprising since, in approximately the past seven decades, the British and Europeans have concentrated on the Tuberous types, whilst the Americans have been preoccupied with other begonias, reflecting the climatic differences between Europe and America. The truth of this finding is evident in the content of *The Begonian* (published by the American Begonia Society) and the Bulletins of the National Begonia Society and the Scottish Begonia Society.

In part, the almost exclusive interest in Tuberous begonias in Britain has been due to the difficulty in obtaining many examples of Non-tuberous begonia plants. This situation is slowly changing partly because plants from America can now be in a British greenhouse within four or five days of leaving the American supplier, and also because more and more nurseries both within Britain and the EC (European Community) are taking an interest in selling begonias of the foliage type.

The ease with which plant material can be sent into Britain from an EC country has considerably increased. It is now possible to import up to five plants without a health certificate as a 'baggage concession'. However, by far the greatest selection of Non-tuberous begonias is in America, although rapid strides are being made in Australia, and the supply is now readily available to growers in Britain.

This book deals with the practical cultivation of a broad range of begonias and lists, in the main, those varieties and species available to varying degrees in Britain, Europe and America. (More extensive lists of Non-tuberous begonias, most of which can be bought in America, are available elsewhere.)

BEGONIA CLASSIFICATION

Classification still poses difficulties since no one approach is universally accepted. The botanical classification, whilst of great value to botanists, is of little interest to amateur begonia growers.

Since this book is primarily concerned with the practice of growing begonias, rather than with a botanical study of the genus, I shall adopt the American horticultural classification with a very slight modification. (In Britain it is the usual practice to describe begonias as either Tuberous or Fibrous-rooted. This is clearly incorrect since, whilst all Tuberous begonias have fibrous roots, not all Fibrous-rooted begonias have tubers.)

The American system subdivides the begonia family into eight groups: Cane-like, Semperflorens, Rhizomatous, Rex cultorum, Tuberous, Trailing-scandent, Shrub-like, and Thick-stemmed. I shall deal with examples of the first five (separately examining Hiemalis and Cheimantha types in the Tuberous section), and select only a small number of Shrub-like and the Thick-stemmed begonias for discussion. The cultivation of a limited number of Non-tuberous begonias is given in outline only. Other texts (*see* Appendix IV) will have to be consulted for greater detail on the wider range of known species and hybrids, together with their cultivation.

Some begonias are ideal subjects for greenhouse cultivation, others can make very attractive houseplants, whilst still others are valuable subjects for the garden. Some of the begonias discussed may be used satisfactorily in more than one of the above applications. Also, note that when discussing Tuberous begonias some books tend to refer only to the named, large-flowered, Tuberous, double types, whereas I shall include the other available Tuberous types (Crispa marginata, Marmorata, etc.)

NATIONAL FAVOURITES

It is interesting to observe that the word 'begonia' conjures up different images depending upon which country one happens to be in. For instance in Britain the majority of people equate begonias with the exotic looking flowers often seen at the various horticultural summer shows because relatively few Non-tuberous begonias are cultivated there. Indeed, by far the greatest percentage of the membership of both the National Begonia Society and the Scottish Begonia Society grow only the Tuberous double types. In America the cultivation of Tuberous begonias is almost restricted to northern California and the eastern states, whilst in Australia this type of begonia is largely confined to a relatively small area around Adelaide. The excessively hot summers and warm winters in the remainder of Australia and America make the cultivation of Tuberous begonias a non-starter. In general, growers concentrate on the types of begonia which are most readily cultivated in their climatic conditions and ignore those which pose a greater challenge.

Incidentally, detailed historical accounts of the development of begonias are not provided since they can be found in other publications. Nevertheless, some historical information will be included since it provides a better understanding of the growing conditions required by the various begonias.

BEGONIA CULTIVATION

Over the years begonia cultivation has changed very little. The most significant development has been the almost 100 per cent switch from loam-based to peat-based composts. Minor changes do occur from time to time concerning watering and feeding procedures, but these issues tend to be somewhat cyclical, coming and going like most fashions.

As with the cultivation of any plant, no two growers use exactly identical techniques. There is always some difference concerning, for example, the amount and frequency of watering, intensity of light, the precise composition of the growing medium, and so on. These are also issues which one cannot (nor would one wish to) define, stressing that successful growing is still more of an art than a science. Consequently I shall discuss as many approaches as possible, in detail. In fact I have two goals. The first is to help people grow better begonias, and the second is to introduce readers to other types of begonia. (Readers would be well advised to visit the many specialist begonia shows and exhibitions to see for themselves the huge range of plants available.) If one objective is achieved that will be a fine reward, and if both are realized that indeed will be a bonus.

1
SEMPERFLORENS BEGONIAS

There seems little doubt that Begonia x semperflorens (commonly known as Semps) is the most popular and widely grown begonia in the world. Throughout Europe and America many many thousands of these colourful and floriferous bedding subjects are cultivated annually. And during the summer months they can be seen in every town and city in massed bedding displays in public parks and gardens.

Generally speaking they are available either as fairly low-growing plants 6–8in (15–20cm) high, or as taller plants measuring some 10–12in (25–30cm) in height. The flower colours range from white, through pale pink to salmon-orange and bright red. Even some bicolours are available, but unfortunately no yellow variety as yet exists. This display of bright, cheery flower colours is often enhanced by the glossy green or bronze-mahogany foliage occasionally covered in fine white or grey hairs. These are the single-flowered Semperflorens begonias grown *en masse* to create a carpet of colour, but also available are several varieties with semi-double, or double-flowers, and even a few with variegated leaves carrying white or yellow splashes on the green background. As we shall see these latter types of Semperflorens are really unsuitable for outdoor use particularly in Britain.

Though undoubtedly the major use of the single-flowered Semperflorens begonias is as bedding plants, nevertheless selected examples do lend themselves to cultivation as most attractive pot plants in the house, cool greenhouse, or conservatory. They are relatively easy to manage and will repay the effort with year-long flowering. They can be used very effectively as patio plants, and one or two can be used as most useful and attractive plants for hanging baskets.

The history of this group of begonias goes back a little over 100 years, and may be traced to the plant's introduction into Europe and the crossing of two South American species. The first in *B. semperflorens*, a fairly tall-growing species from Brazil which has dark green leaves covered in white hairs, and which produces small white flowers especially in summer. The second is *B. schmidtiana*, another Brazilian species, but which is a shorter growing plant with dark green leaves covered with fine greyish hairs. The small flowers are pale pink, profusely but only infrequently borne.

The hybrids produced from these two species were soon being crossed with a third *B. roezlii* (*B. bracteosa*), which is also South American and tall growing at 24in (60cm), but with brilliant scarlet-red flowers in winter/spring. This cross produced taller hybrids but also increased the colour range into the deeper pinks and red, as well as extending the flowering season. Later on further hybridization with such species as *B. fuchsiodes* gave rise to varieties with much smaller, glossy leaves.

Considerable development has continued since those early times, especially in Denmark, Germany, and America, to produce the wide range of quality hybrids available today. The cultivars presently being distributed are stable because they come true to colour from seed.

The cultivars with bronze-mahogany and variegated foliage are most probably mutants, but nevertheless they are also stable. Many of the semi-double, and double-flowered varieties were developed in America by the firm Logees, but interestingly enough one of the earliest B. x 'Gustav Lind' (commonly known as 'Lund') is reputed to be a cross of *B. semperflorens* with B. x tuberhybrida. Yet just how reliable this statement is cannot be ascertained since a 1950 report by Butterfield describes this variety as a Swedish cross of *B. semperflorens* with *B. fuchsiodes*.

It should also be noted that although in a recent catalogue one of the French nurseries was listing three 'Gustav' varieties – white, pink and red – the major source of the double and semi-doubles is still America.

CULTIVATION

In general the cultivation of the Semperflorens cultorum group is fairly straightforward, but here we shall consider pot plant cultivation separately from outdoor bedding. All the single-flowered Semperflorens are grown from seed, though propagation of individual varieties can also be achieved from cuttings. On the other hand, since it is extremely difficult to obtain seed of the semi-double and double varieties, or those with variegated foliage, then these are invariably propagated from cuttings and plants have to be purchased.

Outdoor Cultivation

Semperflorens seed can be obtained from quite a number of seedsmen. It is selected on the basis of flower and leaf colour, as well as the intended use of the plants. If, for instance, they are to be used as edging plants for beds and borders the dwarfer 6–8in (15–20cm) varieties will clearly be the best choice. However, the taller varieties are obviously the preferred choice for subjects intended for positions further back in the beds. Both types are ideal subjects for use in tubs and patio containers. Many of the Semperflorens sold today are the very vigorous and floriferous F1 hybrids.

Although such begonias are far more tolerant of good light conditions than many others, they still do not like intense, direct sunlight. The bronze-mahogany leaved varieties are somewhat less susceptible to scorch than the green-leaved types, but even so it is far better to provide suitable light and dappled shade at the height of summer. Semperflorens begonias are also far more tolerant of both damp and dry conditions, but nevertheless they will not thrive in heavy, wet soils. The sappy stems are very vulnerable to botrytis, and once this occurs it is very difficult to prevent the whole plant from collapsing.

The site needs to be well prepared with humus and good drainage material such as sand, grit, or pea-size gravel before the seedlings are planted in early June. A fertilizer such as Growmore should also have been dug into the top 5in (13cm) at the rate of 2oz per square yard (64g per square m). If the plants are to be grown in outdoor containers then the compost described in Chapter 15 would be ideal. The container should be filled with drainage material (small stones or gravel) to within 5in (13cm) of the top, and the remainder should be filled with growing compost.

Semperflorens seed is similar to that of almost all begonias and requires the same treatment. Since the seed is extremely fine (like red pepper) some care must be taken lest a sneeze blows it away.

The method of seed sowing is common to most begonias and applies to all of the begonias discussed in this text. Similarly the seed sowing compost used throughout this book is described in Chapter 15. It is, however, necessary to stress that the temperature of the seed compost needs to be 65–70°F (18.5–21°C) for successful germination. Assuming that the seed is viable, then the success rate of germination is related to the temperature of the seed bed. At low temperatures the rate is low, but it rises with an increase in temperature passing through a maximum, and then falling sharply as the temperature continues to rise even higher. This applies to the majority of seeds, but with begonias the maximum rate appears to be around 70°F (21°C).

It is important to note that since seed sowing normally takes place from January to March in Britain, the usual method involves preparing a heated sand bed in which a thermostatically controlled heating cable is buried, with the seed tray sitting on top. This mass of sand, which can be as much as 1cwt (50.8kg) or more, must also be brought up to this temperature.

Quite frequently in winter there are fine sunny days when the internal temperature of a greenhouse can soar to around 87°F (30.5°F). The surface temperature of the heated sand bed can also rise quickly up to 95°F (35°C), but germination will not take place at such high temperatures. However, electrically heated propagators which do not rely on a mass of sand will not suffer such violent swings in temperature thereby allowing the seeds to germinate in a relatively stable heat range. Yet even if the seeds successfully germinate, care must also be taken to provide an equally stable temperature so that no check to growth occurs either from cold or excessively hot conditions. For example, there is a thermostatically controlled electric blanket which effectively deals with the above problem. The heating blanket (polyester) is placed on a slab of foamed polystyrene and covered with a sheet of heavy-duty polythene. The plants or seed trays are placed on the polythene sheet, and the whole unit is quite safe since it operates on low voltage. At the end of the season the blanket can be washed down with a sterilizing agent before being rolled up and stored.

The Seedlings

As we have noted, begonia seed is so fine that if it is sown undiluted the seedlings will be concentrated into clumps thus making transplanting more difficult than is necessary. It is therefore normal to dilute the seed by mixing it with four or five times its volume of dry silver sand or finely sieved vermiculite. This not only helps to thin out the germinated seedlings but assists in reducing the possibility of fungal infections. Begonia seed germinates when it has the correct amount of warmth, moisture and light, so the seed trays are covered with a sheet of glass only to conserve humidity. The large temperature difference between the compost and the greenhouse will cause water droplets to form overnight on the underside of the glass. These droplets must be wiped off each morning to prevent them falling on to the compost surface.

The seed is sown on the compost surface and settled by a light

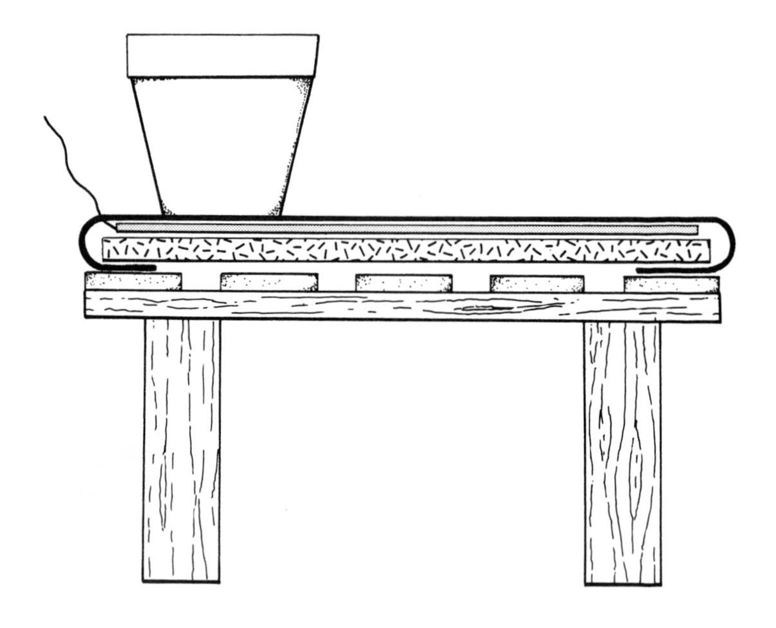

Propagator using electrically heated blanket.

spraying with clean water. From now on the compost should be kept just moist but not too wet. Under optimum conditions germination could take place within four days, but up to one month is more normal under less satisfactory circumstances. At the first sign of germination the glass is removed to prevent the seedlings being 'drawn'.

Begonia seedlings are extremely small and their subsequent growth is not very rapid. Whilst the seedlings are tiny they are also susceptible to damping off caused by fungal infection, and to reduce this possibility the compost is kept moist by immersion watering. The presence of the silver sand will also help to reduce the tendency for the seedlings to damp off, but nevertheless it can still sometimes occur. There are two ways of preventing fungal infection. First, incorporate a fungicide (such as Cheshunt Compound) into the water. Dissolve about 1oz (28g) in warm water and then add to 2gal (9l) of cold water. An alternative is the fungicide Filex. The second method involves 'pasteurizing' the sowing medium before sowing the seed. This will be dealt with later in Chapter 15.

Transplanting is carried out when the second and true seedling leaves have appeared. This is a task which calls for great care and patience since even at this stage the seedlings are extremely small. A cocktail stick or alternatively a 5in (13cm) length of a plastic knitting needle is useful for loosening the seedling before lifting it, carefully holding a leaf to avoid damaging the fleshy stems.

Proceed in this way and transplant the seedlings 2in (5cm) apart in a tray containing a 3in (7.5cm) depth of seed compost. At this stage the seedlings should be kept at about 60–65°F (16–18.5°C) in good, but not direct, sunlight since the seedlings scorch very easily. The compost needs to be moist but not too wet, and feeding should be carried out regularly using a diluted, balanced, liquid feed applied to the foliage as a very fine spray every third day. When the seedlings reach some 3in (7.5cm) in height, but before planting outdoors, the growing tip of each plant should be removed to encourage the plant to branch. Since it normally takes some four months from germination to planting out, there is ample time to prepare the site where they are to flower.

It must be stressed that care should be taken about the choice of site if one is going to get the best out of these begonias. Though direct sunlight is a problem they must not be grown in dense shade or they will become leggy and deficient in flowers. Light shading provided by taller plants can be most helpful.

Most of the modern Semperflorens begonias do have a natural branching habit, but pinching out the growing tips will ensure a more compact and bushier plant. 'Keep on pinching' is a good maxim as far as the cultivation of Semperflorens is concerned.

Because Semperflorens are such floriferous subjects many dead flowers will fall during a season and, if not removed, will greatly encourage pests and diseases (particularly botrytis) which will reduce the vigour of the plants. Even out of doors, and particularly during a dry or even a continuously wet spell, Semperflorens begonias are prone to mildew which is evident as a white powdery material on the stems or leaves. If this is seen then an immediate spraying with a fungicide is essential – one containing Dinocap (for example PBI Multirose), or alternatively Nimrod-T, are very effective.

Pot Plant Cultivation

Semperflorens begonias make the most attractive and valuable pot plants suitable both for the greenhouse and the home. Given the right temperatures, and the necessary amount of light, they can quite easily flower virtually all the year round. They are particularly adaptable as houseplants since their demands in respect of atmospheric humidity are extremely modest, even where central heating is installed. The variegated leaf and the double varieties are particularly attractive, indeed some of the latter types appear to have far more flowers than leaves. However the single-flowered varieties, more usually seen outdoors, should not be ignored.

Semperflorens are not deep-rooted plants and will often perform best if cultivated in half pots. Furthermore, because of their susceptibility to stem rot it is advisable to use clay pots rather than the plastic variety. Other decorative containers may be used as long as the compost can dry out fairly quickly.

The compost can be either John Innes No 2 loam-based, or a peat-based type, both requiring extra grit or perlite to increase the drainage rate. The composts described in Chapter 15 are quite satisfactory. A temperature of 60–70°F (16–21°C) is ideal for the cultivation of Semperflorens begonias, but significant fluctuations outside these limits can result in a check to the rate of growth. Incidentally, atmospheric humidity can be as low as 50 per cent (relative humidity), since these begonias are quite tolerant in this respect.

The plants need to be given as much light as possible without direct sunlight since they scorch very easily where there is no air movement to cool the leaf surfaces. In the northern hemisphere where winter sunshine can sometimes be at a premium, and the day length is short, the plants can be kept growing by supplementing both the intensity and the length of daylight by fluorescent lighting. Two fluorescent tubes each 2ft (60cm) long, placed some 6–9in (15–23cm) above the plants could satisfactorily illuminate an area of 2 × 2ft (60 × 60cm) and would be extremely economical to run.

As the plants continue to grow it is constantly essential to pinch out the growing tips, the stem being removed just above a side shoot. This will greatly assist in building up a very bushy plant, partly by branching but also by encouraging new growths to appear from the base of the plant (though note that certain varieties, such as the 'Olympia' series, do produce more basal growths than do other cultivars).

We have already noted the susceptibility of Semperflorens begonias to the possibility of rotting when kept under wet conditions. The use of clay pots will help to reduce this, as will watering only when it is necessary. Indeed, it is better to err on the side of underwatering whilst realizing this does not mean that begonias should be cultivated under drought conditions. Watering is necessary only when the top layers of the compost – say ½–¾in (13–20mm) below the surface – have completely dried out. The danger is not just overwatering but also providing too little. The latter will seriously inhibit the development of the plants, as will be clearly seen in the state of the leaves. With insufficient water the foliage takes on a silvery sheen, a sure indicator that something needs to be done quickly if the death of the plant is to be avoided.

Inside a greenhouse or the home, powdery mildew can become a problem, and a careful watch should be kept for the appearance of the tell-tale ash-like spots on the leaves and stems. A very light spraying with dilute fungicide (for example one containing Dinocap and Benlate) when the first signs appear will be helpful in controlling this disease.

Particularly during the spring and summer months the plants require feeding with a balanced fertilizer (such as NPK 20:20:20) every three weeks using one-quarter strength. If growth appears to slow down (with other conditions satisfactory) then raising the nitrogen content of the feed will help (NPK 30:10:10). If there appears to be a reluctance to flower then change to a high potash formulation (NPK 12:12:35) again at one-quarter strength. During the long flowering season, using regular applications of fertilizer, there will develop a build-up of harmful salts in the compost which must be removed by periodical application of clear water. This needs to be done only perhaps on three occasions during the season. Though the smaller varieties of Semperflorens will need no support the taller ones will benefit from staking. The time will inevitably come when the plants need repotting, and at this stage the next size pot only should be selected since Semperflorens seem to be far better for being slightly root-bound.

PROPAGATION

It has already been noted that the single-flowered varieties are most readily propagated from seed. Today it is quite possible to purchase the F1 hybrids in specific colour ranges – for example 'Dancia Red', 'Olympia White', 'Pink Avalanche', etc., as well as mixed colours. If one has no facilities for seed sowing then most of the seed nurseries do sell small plantlets in a restricted choice of varieties.

Single-flowered Semperflorens can be propagated from cuttings, though this is not too satisfactory. Such cuttings should be taken as far down the plant as possible and should preferably be one of the main stems. The shoot taken should already have branched since this helps to ensure that the rooted cutting will also retain this branching habit. The cutting should be about 4–5in (10–13cm) long, and be rooted in a suitable compost for cuttings.

The variegated foliage and double-flowered Semperflorens begonias are always propagated from cuttings taken as described above, and usually in early spring. With the variegated foliage types it is essential to ensure that the cutting chosen should have leaves which show at least 50 per cent green pigmentation.

By far the most satisfactory method, however, for all types of Semperflorens propagation involves splitting the mature plant into two or three pieces in late summer, and potting each piece separately.

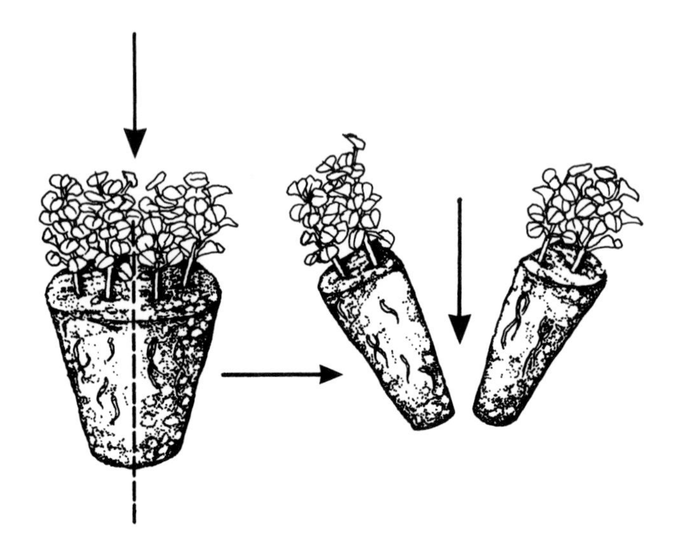

Dividing a Semperflorens plant. The mature plant is propagated by dividing the plant into two halves using a sharp knife.

VARIETIES

There is a long, exciting list of Semperflorens begonias, and it is being added to every year. The list below is intended only as a guide and in no way is it exhaustive, merely representative. The double-types (including variegated foliage kinds) are more commonly available in America, but can easily be exported to other countries.

A. Single-Flowered Varieties

Green leaved	Bronze/mahogany leaved
Tall	
'Frilly' series	'Galaxy' series
'Pink Avalanche'	'Danica Red'
'Wings-mixed'	'Danica Rose'
'Mars'	'Othello'
'Salina'	'Musk Rose'
'Loveliness'	
Dwarf	
'Olympia White'	'Indian Maid'
'Scarletta'	'Karin'
'Olympia Salmon Orange'	'Saga'
'Thousand Wonders'	'Galaxy' series
'Organdy' series	'Volcano'
'Olympia Red'	'Devon Gems'
	'Coco Ducolour'

B. Semi-Double and Double

Green foliage	Bronze/Red foliage
'Gustav Lind' – pink	'Ballet' – white
'Dainty Maid' – blush pink	
'Pink Wonder'	
'Snow White'	'Lucy Locket' – pink
'Gustav Blanc'	'Ernest K' – rose red
'Gustav Rose'	'Gustav Rouge'

Note: Included in Group B are a few varieties which the Americans call 'Thimble' hybrids. The flowers are thimble-shaped, and the flowers appear crested as the partially modified stamens provide a vivid colour contrast to the flower petals. Three worth mentioning are:

'Cinderella': Pink blooms edged with cherry red, and a yellow crest.
'Goldielocks': Pink petals with yellow inside and light bronze foliage.
'Pied Piper': A dwarf plant with crested pink flowers and very dark foliage.

C. Variegated Foliage

'Calla Lily': Red flowers, leaves green and white.
'Charm': Pink flowers, leaves green with white and gold splashes.
'Cherry Sundae': Cherry red flowers, leaves pure white and green.

There is little doubt that the Semperflorens group of begonias are most versatile and valuable. They provide impressive banks of colour in garden displays, make attractive patio plants, are fairly tolerant of periods of either wet or dry weather, and can be cultivated as flowering houseplants able to withstand and even thrive in centrally-heated homes.

2
HIEMALIS AND CHEIMANTHA BEGONIAS

As we shall see later the Tuberous begonias are essentially summer-flowering plants, with the tubers requiring a winter period of dormancy of four to five months. This is a characteristic inherited from their Andean ancestry and has remained an important differentiating (and some would say undesirable) feature of the whole range of Tuberous begonias.

HIEMALIS BEGONIAS

Just over 100 years ago two new begonia species were introduced into Europe from South Africa. They were *B. socotrana* – from the island of Socotra in the Indian Ocean off the west African coast. (A bulbous species which flowers in the winter from December to February.) And *B. dregei* – from South Africa. (A semi-tuberous species which flowered from late summer into the autumn, producing a mass of small white flowers.)

Hybridists of the time, both in Europe and Britain, were quick to appreciate that here was a possibility of developing a new breed of winter-flowering cultivars. The very earliest crosses were of *B. socotrana* with a number of Tuberous hybrids available at the time. The products of these crosses were given the name Hiemalis begonias and, while they retained some of the desirable characteristics of the summer-flowering types, such as fairly large flowers and succulent stems, the flowering season was much extended and they no longer had a dormancy period.

Though strictly named B. x hiemalis, nevertheless they are more commonly known in America as Clibran begonias, and elsewhere as Elatior begonias. They are not widely grown today though certainly until a few years ago a number were still available, for example 'Altringham Pink', 'Emily Clibran', 'Gloire de Sceaux' and 'Exquisite'. These Hiemalis begonias were dwarf, bushy plants, and were amongst the very first to be known as winter-flowering. They grew well under fluorescent light but great care was needed in watering procedures. Occasionally the fibrous roots would develop swollen sections reminiscent of their tuberous parentage. Considerable difficulty was experienced keeping these early varieties through the winter which contributed to their loss of favour as houseplants. The commercial growers soon began to cross *B. socotrana* with a variety of other begonias, especially the Rhizomatous types. For these hybrids the name Hiemalis-like was chosen because of their close resemblance to the Hiemalis begonias.

During the period up to about 1936 the major developments in this group were made in Holland and England, but then the beginning of the Second World War prevented further work. However, after 1945 a whole new breed of Hiemalis-like begonias were developed, capable of producing many more flowers, single and double, and in a much wider colour range. They are generally known by the name of the German who carried out much of the original work, Otto Rieger. These Rieger begonias (frequently called Elatior begonias) are now widely available in florists' shops, large retail outlets and garden centres. Some new varieties have also been developed in America by Mikkelsens of Ohio.

Today there is still the tendency to treat the Rieger begonias almost as annual plants, and indeed it can be assumed that by far the greatest percentage of these plants sold today are kept in the home until flowering is over when they are thrown away. With some care however, they can be kept successfully through the winter. The Riegers can be readily recognized by the 2½–3in (6.5–8cm) size glossy leaves in shades of dark green to bronze. The plants are very free flowering and produce a multitude of 1½in (4cm) single, semi-double and double-blooms in vibrant colours of red, yellow, orange and pink, as well as white and even bicolours and picotees. It would be quite wrong to suggest that the double-flowers had the perfection of form of the large-flowered, Tuberous, doubles (there is no valid reason why they should), but we are clearly at the beginning of a whole new race of the Hiemalis-like begonias.

Cultivation

In Britain and probably the rest of Europe the Hiemalis-like or Elatior begonias are invariably purchased in bloom as unnamed plants at most florists, and at many of the supermarket outlets usually from March onwards. One or two nurseries in Britain do list a selection of named varieties, though such has been the speed of development of these begonias during the past decade that it is doubtful if the extra expense they incur is justified. The unnamed plants are normally selected on the basis of their flower colour, and the usual practice is to buy the plant still in its 2–3in (5–7.5cm) pot which is buried intact in an outer 5–6in (13–15cm) pot. Occasionally the grower has opened up the sides of the inner pot to allow root development to take place into the larger pot, but this is by no means the general experience.

If the intention is to treat the plant merely as a houseplant, to be disposed of at the end of the flowering season, then it is probably best to leave it undisturbed, give it plenty of light but no direct sun, keep it fed and watered and in a warm place, about 55°F (13°C) minimum. Any liquid, balanced fertilizer will suit the purpose, but it is essential that the plant does not remain wet for any length of time. Keeping a watchful eye on the development of the plant will tell you what is needed: a reluctance to maintain flowering is probably due to the light level being too low, whereas growth which is too leggy is most probably due to excessively heavy feeding made even worse by insufficient light.

Specimen Plants

If, however, the intention is to grow the plant into a specimen over a number of seasons then the treatment will be somewhat different and correspondingly more difficult. First of all the plant has to be freed from its existing small pot. Elatior begonias do not like too great a root disturbance on being repotted, so this procedure has to be done as carefully as possible. The roots are then very gently teased slightly apart to allow them to grow into the new compost. The plant is potted on into the next size pot. A very open compost must be used for the Elatior or Rieger begonias – it must have a high air-filled porosity so that the plants avoid having their root system constantly wet, a situation which will undoubtedly result in root rot. A possible alternative to this treatment, and one often practised in nurseries, involves leaving the original small pot in place but carefully cutting away large segments of it using a sharp knife or scissors, and then moving the plant into a larger size pot.

Split cane stakes about 1ft (30cm) long are then placed around the circumference of the pot.

The plant is now given the maximum amount of light, but out of direct sunlight, and the air temperature is kept as far as possible within 60–65°F (16–18.5°C).

Plant Care

This type of begonia is not too demanding as far as atmospheric humidity is concerned, preferring a good circulation of air around the leaves. The growth habit of these begonias is such that a lot of succulent stems are congested within a small area and, unless there is plenty of air movement, they will suffer attacks of botrytis. This type of disease is also encouraged if the spent blooms are allowed to fall on to the foliage and remain there. In order to reduce the risk of rot, and to encourage further blooms, all dead flowers should be removed as quickly as possible. Though botrytis can be controlled using fungicide sprays it is far better to avoid it.

The same is true of mildew which can also be quite a problem. Prevention is far preferable to cure and a low humidity of 40–45 per cent will help. At the first sign of botrytis the area should be fumigated using a Tecnazine smoke cone, and similarly if mildew appears it is better to use a smoke cone before resorting to a spray.

The plants should be watered and fed only when the compost shows clear indications of drying out, but when watered the compost must be thoroughly wetted and the excess allowed to drain away. Feeding should take place in the season of fast growth using a reliable liquid feed at about one-half the recommended strength, and at intervals of three weeks. A suitable NPK value for the fertilizer should be either 20:20:20, or perhaps 12:12:35, during a particularly heavy flowering period.

The Rieger begonias will reward care and attention by producing masses of bloom throughout the summer, and into the autumn, when there will be a noticeable reduction in the number of flowers being produced. The way to encourage winter-flowering is by ensuring that the plants get a good 12 hours darkness a day throughout October and November. In the darker days from December to March it helps if you can provide the plants with artificial light so that they receive 10–12 hours good quality light per day. A similar arrangement to that described for Semperflorens (*see* page 10) is adequate. It has to be admitted, however, that bringing a plant which has completely stopped flowering back into bloom in the spring is not always easy, and is more difficult with the single-flowered varieties (which seem to need a higher light level) than the doubles.

In April and May, or mid to late spring, new growths will appear at the base of the plant when some of the old growths should be cut back to 2–3in (5–7.5cm) long. The plant should also be knocked from its pot to check if it is necessary to move it to a larger size. At this stage much of the old root ball should be shaken off and the plant repotted into fresh compost. In many instances it is possible to repot into the same size pot. Providing a bottom heat of about 65°F (18.5°C) will get the new growth off to a good start.

Many growers do find great difficulty in bringing the Rieger begonias successfully through the winter, losses occurring usually because the compost is kept too wet resulting in rotting. During the winter very little water is required (if any), and the plants can manage quite well for a week or two without watering. Again the foliage will tell you when more water is needed, with the leaves going limp and beginning to droop. Very little water, a warm environment, and as good a light as possible will assist greatly in overwintering these begonias.

However, to guard against the possible demise of the plant propagation is a necessity and is usually carried out with cuttings taken in late spring.

Propagation

The detailed accounts of propagation will be given in Chapter 13 and it is sufficient here to say that stocks of the Hiemalis-like begonias can be increased by stem cuttings, basal cuttings, or leaf cuttings.

The Hiemalis-like and Rieger begonias are notoriously reluctant to produce seed, indeed the vast majority of blooms on these plants are males. Nevertheless the seedsmen do occasionally offer Elatior seed and, though quite expensive to purchase, it is worth trying to grow. The one being offered at the present time is 'Charisma', which produces large 2in (5cm) diameter, double-blooms in shades of orange to coral. The seeds are sown from January–March, and germinate at a temperature of 65–70°F (18.5–21°C), the seedling plants being grown on in the way described for all begonia plants. When grown from seed the resulting seedlings tend to grow with a single stem, and rarely produce a bushy plant during the first year. During November most will most probably cease blooming. To overcome both conditions it is sensible to begin pinching out the growing points as soon as the seedling is growing well, in order to force more basal growth and branching. This procedure will help to produce a plant with far more flower, and one which has a greater chance of remaining in bloom through the winter.

Varieties

Hiemalis-Like

Whilst these varieties are quite rare they are well worth seeking out.

'Altringham Pink': Fully double pink and Christmas flowering.
'Emily Clibran': Large, double, salmon-pink.
'Gloire de Sceaux': Rose-pink blooms, bronze foliage.
'Nelly Visser': Early, scarlet rosebud blooms.

Elatior or Rieger

In Britain it is most unusual to find named varieties on sale, and selection is on the basis of colour. However, a few named ones are listed here and can be obtained from at least one supplier.

'Aphrodite' series: Double flowers in a series of colours.
'Baluga' series: Scarlet red with green foliage and single flowers.
'Elfe': Almost a picotee with a cream base, edged pink.
'Krefeld' series: As 'Baluga', but with bronze leaves.
'Melody' series: White, red and yellow, single flowers very freely produced.

CHEIMANTHA BEGONIAS

Though undoubtedly the Hiemalis-type have a much longer flowering period than many other begonias, nevertheless they are not truly winter-flowering plants. However, crossing the two African species *B. socotrana* and *B. dregei* gave rise to the hybrid 'Gloire de Lorraine' which is capable of producing flowers through the winter from November to January. Most of the 1in (2.5cm) diameter pink flowers are male and sterile which means propagation involving cuttings.

For many years after its introduction 'Gloire de Lorraine' was produced commercially and in great quantity. Its popularity has somewhat declined in recent years because it is rather difficult for amateur growers to cultivate, requiring a temperature of 55–60°F (13–16°C) to maintain winter growth. Since the introduction of the first Christmas-flowering begonia, or 'Lorraine' begonia – or more correctly Cheimantha begonia – a number of sports of 'Gloire de Lorraine' have been produced and propagated by cuttings. Generally the colour range has been pink, white or red.

Though the male flowers are sterile and the female blooms are produced very sparingly at the end of the flowering season, a few backcrosses have been produced by using the pollen of *B. socotrana*. This has led to some varieties with increased vigour and a greater range of leaf colour. Within this group of Cheimantha-like begonias are a number of crosses of *B. socotrana* with begonias other than *B. dregei* – for instance *B. herbacea*. Today there are few cultivars in this group still grown, and they are likely to be found in the hands of amateur enthusiasts. However, in the last few years it has become possible to obtain F1 seed of a Cheimantha begonia named 'Love Me'. All the Cheimantha and Cheimantha-like begonias are tuberous.

Cultivation

The method of taking cuttings will be dealt with in Chapter 13, and growing from seed is identical to the method described for Semperflorens in Chapter 1. Here one assumes that either small seedlings or rooted cuttings are available in early April. These are potted into 2in (5cm) pots using a normal potting compost described in Chapter 15. The young plants are grown on at around 60°F (16°C).

Cheimantha begonias need to have their growing points continually pinched out to assist in creating a bushy plant structure. They also require potting on fairly frequently, say three or four times between April and August, the objective being to finish up in a 4–5in (10–13cm) diameter pot. Each time potting on occurs it helps to place the newly potted plant on a heated sand bench, encouraging as rapid a development of the root system as possible. If a number of plants are available then the flowering season may be somewhat extended by ceasing the pinching process for some in August, and for others in September. The plants should be fed every week throughout the summer using a balanced fertilizer at half strength. In September the plants are placed out of direct sunlight, but where the temperature can be kept at 60°F (16°C). The atmospheric humidity should be kept on the low side, at about 40–50 per cent, and a careful watch maintained for any sign of mildew or insect pest.

Cheimantha begonias prefer to be grown slightly on the dry side since too frequent watering is extremely bad for them. It is also quite usual to grow two or three plants in a slightly larger 5in (13cm) pot to provide an even bigger flower display.

Varieties

As has been indicated a wide range of 'Lorraine' begonias is available in America, although they are harder to locate elsewhere. This is true of the varieties listed below.

'Curly Cloud': A cross between *B. socotrana* and 'Bokit'.
'Gloire de Lorraine': The original Cheimantha begonia with pink flowers profusely borne (and available in Britain).
'Love Me': An F1 hybrid grown from seed, producing small coral pink flowers produced in abundance.
'Marjorie Gibbs': Purplish-pink flowers.
'Pink African Violet': A deep pink flowering plant with a long flowering season; it is a cross of *B. socotrana* with *B. herbacea*.
'Red Solfheim': Very profuse flowering plant with cerise-coloured blooms.

3
TUBEROUS BEGONIAS

The common characteristics of the begonias described in this, and the following three chapters, are that they all form tubers and each has an annual dormant or resting period. In Britain this is roughly November/December to February/March, but in the Southern Hemisphere it is more usually April to August. This reversal of seasons is an important consideration when importing stock from the Southern to the Northern Hemisphere. For example, since the Australian growing season (October–April) coincides with the British dormant period (November–April), it may well be necessary to refrigerate the tubers at about 40°F (4.5°C) to prevent the tubers starting into growth until the correct seasonal sequence has been established.

Since Tuberous begonias have a dormant period which coincides with the British winter they are essentially late summer-flowering subjects. Within this group of Tuberous begonias a number of sub-groups may be identified based upon the flower form and plant habit. For example here, and in the following three chapters, we shall be considering the large-flowered Tuberous doubles, Pendulas and Cascades, the Multiflora types, and the single-flowered varieties. All have been developed from the same four or five Tuberous species, and all may be cultivated under the same basic conditions. The fact that certain Tuberous begonias are cultivated under the protection of a greenhouse or conservatory indicates that the cost of these tubers is very high, and that they can only achieve their full potential under these conditions.

All can be successfully grown outside in the garden or on a patio, and indeed a cool, moist spring and autumn, together with a warm (not hot) summer is ideal for the cultivation of tuberous begonias. Indeed, the habitat of the original species, high in the Andes mountains of South America, seems to be more closely allied to the temperate areas of Europe than to the arid and the tropical parts of the world.

Begonia cultivation, as discussed here, is normally from tubers purchased from January onwards from garden centres, nurseries, and even some supermarket retail outlets. By far the largest percentage of tubers sold are unnamed and are particularly suited to cultivation in the garden. They are usually imported from the bulb growers of Belgium and Holland. The Tuberous begonias which have the greatest potential for large and almost perfect flowers are the named varieties. They are very expensive and are usually only obtainable from specialist nurseries. It must be emphasized, however, that apart from their potential to give large and perfectly formed flowers these varieties do not differ in any substantial way from their much cheaper relations. There is also an increasing number of extremely good, named begonias being made available by amateur hybridists, and in certain instances one could claim that these amateur, named varieties are superior to some of the commercially produced varieties.

A word of warning however, needs to be sounded. The commercial varieties can be seen at shows during the summer, and grown invariably as pot plants when the acceptability of their growth habit can be judged. All too frequently many of the new introductions from amateurs are seen initially as cut blooms and, whilst their plant growth habits might be perfectly satisfactory, this cannot be inferred from the cut bloom alone. The mere fact that a Tuberous begonia carries a name does not in itself guarantee either a quality plant nor, I am afraid, a quality bloom. One needs to be reassured that the variety has been raised and selected by a nursery which has had a long, international, and specialist reputation in this field or, alternatively, that the amateur hybridist also has an acknowledged reputation for producing good quality new cultivars. Because of their high cost, and to avoid any damage from the elements, the named begonias are invariably grown in a greenhouse or in another protective environment.

Tuberous begonias may also be grown from seed sown very early in the year, and at a temperature of some 65–70°F (18.5–21°C). It must be appreciated, however, that the seedlings will need to be grown on for at least three months in an air temperature of no less than 50°F (10°C), requiring supplementary heating before the natural heat of the sun can maintain adequate daily growth. The plants obtained from seed can be grown to maturity either in the greenhouse or in the garden, and will probably produce a few small flowers by September, together with a small tuber. If stored through the winter this tuber may be grown on in the second year to produce a better yield of larger flowers, at which time their true potential may be assessed.

A question frequently asked is, 'How long will begonia tubers last?'. The answer is that we simply do not know. Certainly with some varieties, and with suitable care, tubers can be successfully grown for 10 years or more during which time they may reach some 8in (20cm) in diameter. Other varieties are difficult to keep alive for much longer than three or four years. The general experience, however, is that older tubers do seem to lose some of their vigour so that, not surprisingly, propagation is an important feature of begonia growing.

HISTORY

The history of the Tuberous group of begonias may be traced back to at least five, and perhaps seven Andean species from Bolivia and Peru, and a small but significant contribution from one species from South Africa. They were as follows:

B. cinnabarina
From Bolivia, a tall growing plant with large leaves. The flowers are orange-red and, together with *B. veitchii*, have contributed much to the orange varieties of today. Much of the general growth habit of today's hybrids owes a great deal to this species.

B. boliviensis
Again from Bolivia – the long slender stems bear narrow, petalled, scarlet flowers which are carried on tiny pendulous stalks. This species has been a major contributor to today's pendula begonias.

B. pearcei
Is also Bolivian. It is a compact plant which is notable for the small, velvety dark green leaves and bright yellow flowers. This characteristic leaf runs through all the modern yellow varieties. It is the only yellow species available in this group of begonias.

B. rosaeflora
Is a Peruvian species with pink flowers. A mutant of the species which produced white flowers has been extensively used in the development of the modern white hybrids. It is very likely that this species is synonymous with a fifth species, namely:

B. veitchii
From Peru. This is a fairly small growing species where the flower stalk rises above the foliage and produces orange-red flowers but only sparingly.

B. davisii
Again from Peru, and is a dwarf growing plant with rather hairy, blue-green leaves. The orange flowers are held high above the foliage. This species is an important ancestor of the multiflora group.

B. clarkii
Found in both Bolivia and Peru, and is probably identical to *B. cinnabarina.*

B. dregei
From South Africa. The species has small, red-veined leaves and pure white flowers. Many of the present white-flowered hybrids have *B. dregei* in their ancestry.

In spite of the extensive hybridizing which has taken place in the previous 130 years or so, many of the characteristics of these species can still be seen in today's hybrids. Note, for instance, the weeping habit of *B. boliviensis* in the Pendulas and Cascades, the strong stems of *B. cinnabarina*, the dwarf habit of *B. davisii* in the Multifloras, the velvety green foliage of *B. pearcei* in yellow varieties like 'Primrose' and 'Midas', and the pink pigment showing through some white and yellow varieties like 'Billie Langdon' and 'Lillian Thornton' which is probably due to the influence of *B. rosaeflora* somewhere in the history of these varieties. Many of the true red begonias, such as 'Red Admiral', 'Royalty' and 'Sultan', etc., have very similar foliage in that the reverse of the leaves is reddish, probably deriving from *B. davisii* in the early hybrids.

It is salutary to note that all these species had small 1–1½in (2.5–4cm) diameter single flowers, with many stamens. Since they all flowered at roughly the same time (summer) hybridization posed few problems, and the numerous stamens made the development of double flowers relatively simple. These species were imported into Europe during the period 1860–1870 and soon hybridization was under way in Germany, Belgium, France and England. Within 10 years the first double-flowered hybrid had been obtained, with some of the stamens having been transformed into tepals.

By this time the original botanical interest in begonias had been replaced by a commercial, horticultural one, and it was quickly recognized that most of the then available hybrids had certain undesirable characteristics which resisted all attempts to change. These included weak stems, pendulous flowers and a general drooping habit, and narrow pointed petals.

These undesirable features were present because, up to that time, all the hybridizing had been based on *B. boliviensis* and its initial influence could not be eradicated. A change of direction was needed and, at this stage, attention turned to hybrids based upon the species which had rounded petals and upright flower stems – *B. pearcei* and *B. veitchii*. The subsequent use of *B. boliviensis* in these crosses gave rise to taller plants with circular flowers and strong flower stems, and the further use of *B. cinnabarina* enhanced these characteristics. From this point on careful selection of the plants to be propagated was the main line of development. Indeed, in 1882 one grower laid down his selection criteria as: 'compact and robust habit, large flowers as near circular as possible, the petals rounded and of firm texture, the flower stalk sufficiently stout to show the flower to advantage. The plants should be free flowering.'

At this time the red and pink colours predominated because of the problems associated with whites and yellows. Both these colours had a pronounced tendency for pink shades to show through and indeed 100 years on this tendency is still present in many of today's hybrids in these colours. Some of these early doubles or semi-doubles with their narrow, separated petals resembled the camellia flower, and were appropriately named 'camellia flowered' – a term which, though by now almost meaningless, is still used.

Amongst a batch of seedlings it was noticed that one, a scarlet hybrid, had a form quite distinctly different from the normal camellia type. The petals were broader and overlapping and, in the early stages of development, strongly resembled a rosebud, at that time a completely new form of begonia. Soon the two forms, camellia flowered and the rosebud became the major objectives of the breeders of the time. Today the rosebud-centred begonia (roseform) is looked upon as having the true classical form, whilst the camellia shape has all but disappeared.

From around 1900 to the present day the various breeding programmes followed throughout Europe and America have led to a number of recognizably different groups of Tuberous begonias, of which the following will be discussed here and in the following three chapters: large-flowered doubles; Pendulas and Cascades; Multifloras; others, including Crispa marginata, Fimbriata, Marmorata, etc.

The scientific name given to all these Tuberous hybrids is Begonia x tuberhybrida, or just Tuberhybrida.

LARGE-FLOWERED DOUBLES

In the years following 1900 the development of the large-flowered, Tuberous, double begonias proceeded along two parallel routes. The first involved improving the size and form of the flowers, as well as the plant habit. This was the approach of the English nursery of Blackmore and Langdon and led to the development of selected, named varieties intended for cool greenhouse cultivation.

In America, from around 1935, the firm of Vetterle & Reinelt concentrated their efforts on improving both plant and bloom quality, though not necessarily through the release of named varieties. By careful breeding and selection they made great strides in perfecting the 'roseform' begonias, and introduced the lovely ruffled types (developed from *B. fimbriata plena*) together with the picotee versions of both these forms. A few of their early releases were named, but soon they were simply selecting tubers for sale on the basis of their quality.

The second route involved the development of begonias which could be propagated from seed so that the plants came true to form and colour. This was the line of attack followed in Holland and particularly in Belgium. It led to the mass production of begonia tubers which could be sold by colour, and which had a high probability of being double. By the early 1900s it was possible to obtain begonia seed in every colour, yielding over 90 per cent of double flowers. Today, begonia tubers originating in Europe are sold on a massive scale throughout the world – they show a very high percentage of double flowers, but the quality of the individual blooms cannot be compared with those of the named varieties.

Cultivation

For exhibition work it is essential that named varieties of begonia are purchased or, at the very least; the greenhouse quality unnamed varieties from specialist begonia nurseries. Anything of lesser quality will only lead to disappointment and frustration. Though rather expensive these would also make ideal plants for conservatory use, and as patio plants. For outdoor use (such as bedding plants) or any other type of massed display, then the much cheaper tubers displayed at garden centres, supermarkets, nurseries and garden suppliers, and imported from the continent are adequate. Whether named or unnamed, the dormant tubers are on sale from January onwards, though it is advisable to buy them as early as possible and keep them in store (in a cool but frost-free place) until they require bringing into growth. The named varieties of the large-flowered, Tuberous doubles frequently sell out early in the New Year, so orders need to be placed as soon as possible in the autumn. If suitable facilities are available, such as a heated propagator or sand bench, then plants may be raised from seed (as for Semperflorens – *see* page 7 onwards). The cultivation of Tuberous begonias for exhibition will be covered in Chapter 11.

Using Tubers

On receiving the tubers carefully check for any signs of rot, or other damage, including insect attack. Any area of the tuber which feels either very soft or extremely hard might be infected with rot. Careful removal of a tiny fragment of outer skin at this point will reveal whether rot is present – if it is then the affected area must be cut away completely and the entire cut surface should be dusted with a carbendazim-based fungicide or even green sulphur. (If the tuber is a recently received named variety then the supplier should be immediately notified and the tuber returned.)

Particular attention should be given to the area of the tuber where the previous season's stem was attached. This area will be covered by a tough membrane or callous – in the very moist conditions needed to start the tuber into growth the flesh below this callous may develop rot which can completely destroy the entire tuber. To prevent this, the callous should always be removed by carefully inserting the tip of a penknife blade underneath the edge of the membrane and firmly removing it to expose the clean flesh below. Again the wound should be given a light dusting with sulphur and allowed to dry.

Under normal circumstances the tubers may be kept for a few weeks before being started into growth, provided they are housed in a temperature of not more than about 45°F (7.5°C). At temperatures much above this the tubers will emerge from their dormancy revealing pink growths around the crown. If this occurs too early in the year these growths must be 'rubbed out' before they become too large.

The correct time to start begonia tubers into growth depends on the following: when do you want the plants to flower? is cultivation to be outdoors? or, if in a greenhouse, is there any available heat? For example, if you want your plants to be in flower from August, then, depending on the growing conditions (temperature, humidity, light, feeding, variety, etc.) the starting time will be mid-March. In other words, it usually takes a growing period of five months to bring a begonia to its ideal flowering time. A Tuberous begonia is at its maximum flowering potential when the growths in the leaf axils are flower growths and not side shoots. For most varieties this occurs at about the fourth or fifth leaf. If flowering has to be delayed until the plant has developed six or seven leaves it is becoming too tall and the potential for large flowers will be on the decrease. For August flowering it will be sufficient to start the tubers in late March to early April.

In Britain this will also avoid the need for expensive greenhouse heating through January and February. Flowering much earlier than August would require heat in the first quarter of the year, and possibly the use of fluorescent lighting to enhance both the quality and length of daylight. The Tuberous begonias seen in bloom at the Royal Horticultural Society's show in May are brought into flower by the use of heat and artificial light.

For outdoor use, note that begonias are not particularly frost resistant and cannot be planted out until the end of May or early June, which means a March start. Alternatively, for outdoor bedding use the dormant tubers and plant directly into the ground in mid-April but about 3in (7.5cm) deep to avoid damage from late frosts.

Having decided when to bring the tubers into growth it is a good idea to lay them on a bench 14 days before and spray them daily with clean water. As long as the temperature is above, say, 50°F (10°C) then the moisture does seem to assist in 'plumping up' the tuber before it comes out of dormancy.

Plastic trays or boxes about 4in (10cm) deep make good starting containers. The compost should be the normal growing medium but with added grit to assist drainage (about 1 part grit to 3 parts compost). A 2in (5cm) layer of the compost is placed in a tray, and the tubers are laid on the surface (concave side up) – more compost is then added so that the tubers are covered to a depth of around ½in (13mm). This complete covering with compost is desirable because it encourages root growth from the entire tuber surface, and it prevents water settling on the concave surface and possibly encouraging the onset of wet rot. Each tuber is labelled, the compost well watered and the tray is placed in a heated propagator or on a sand bed. The heating is adjusted so that the compost temperature is 65–70°F (18.5–21°C). It is important to maintain the temperature at or about this range since, if the upper limit is exceeded, growth can be inhibited and root burn can sometimes result.

Tubers in the propagator showing the erratic nature of starting into growth.

Treated in this way most begonias will start into growth in three to four weeks, though there are always one or two which are erratic and might remain in the tray for two months or more before showing any sign of life. The care taken with the harvesting of tubers and their treatment whilst dormant can affect the ease with which they start into growth the following season. Whilst in the starting trays the compost should be watered frequently so that it remains uniformly moist. In practice this watering needs to be done quite frequently (at least every day) since the loss of water from this very free-draining compost at 70°F (21°C) is fairly rapid. It is also very necessary to check the condition of the compost from top to bottom daily, ensuring that it is uniformly moist. Drying out below the tubers easily occurs, inhibiting root development.

At this stage the objective is to produce the maximum root growth possible since without a good root system quality plants cannot be grown. By the time that 2–3in (5–7.5cm) of top growth has developed there should be an adequate root system, justifying moving the plant out of the starting tray. It must be stressed, however, that it is the root development which should be the deciding factor when this move is made. The next stage in cultivation will very much depend upon the use to which the plants are put – garden or greenhouse subjects.

GREENHOUSE CULTIVATION

There is a considerable difference of opinion amongst begonia growers as to how one should proceed at this point. Some experienced growers believe that a first and second potting is essential if good quality plants are to be grown, whilst others, equally firmly, assert that the second potting is quite unnecessary. The need for first and second potting arose because many of the older growers (brought up on cultivating chrysanthemums) became accustomed to packing their loam-based composts fairly tightly around the plants, thus effectively excluding an adequate supply of air both to the medium and to the root system. There was thus a considerable tendency for the compost to become rapidly 'sour', and the second potting became a normal routine practice.

Today, with more open, peat-based composts having the correct air-filled porosity (at 15–20 per cent) together with much looser potting, 'sourness' is a thing of the past and there is no longer any need for the second potting on this account. Today's peat-based composts, properly formulated, can quite easily last the relatively short season of five to six months without experiencing any adverse effect on either its structure or suitability as a growing medium.

Additional feeding, however, is needed. It is also sensible to place the plant slightly lower down in the pot to leave room for top dressing later on. With this in mind the pot, plastic or clay, is selected so that its diameter is about 2in (5cm) greater than the size of the root ball to be accommodated. The plant is placed centrally in the pot on a layer of compost so that a space of 3½–4in (9–10cm) is left from the top of the tuber to the top of the pot. Using these free-draining composts obviates the need for crocks at the bottom of the pot, though growers may choose to continue this practice if they so wish. Compost is poured around the tuber, gently firmed with the fingers and compacted by tapping the pot on the bench until the entire tuber surface is covered. Since there is to be no second potting it is sensible to insert a cane or stake about 2ft (60cm) long immediately behind the stem(s) to be later used as a plant support. A softwood stake ½in (13mm) square, and with a pointed end, is useful and may be rendered much less conspicuous with a suitable timber preservative treatment, or simply by painting it green.

The plant should be given a good watering and placed on the bench in a well-lit position, but shaded from direct sunlight. No

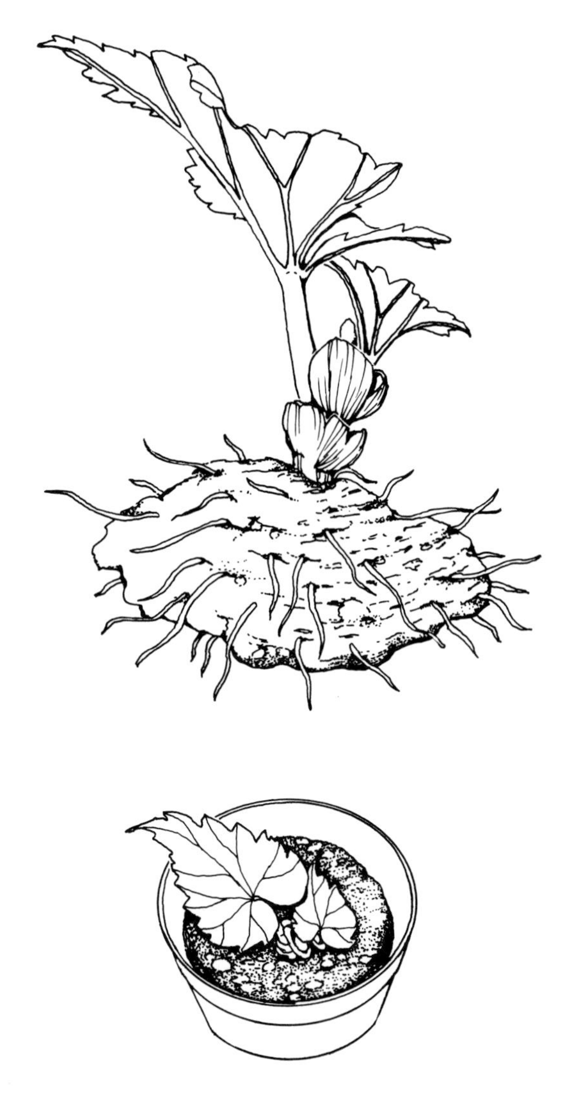

Potting up the tuber.

further watering will be necessary until the compost is on the point of becoming dry. If clay pots are used then the simplest way of determining when to water is to 'ring' the pot. If the pot is tapped and issues a dull, dead sound then no water is required, but a clear ring indicates that water is needed. If plastic pots are being used then it is a little more difficult to estimate the state of the compost – one either has to feel the weight of the pot or check with the fingers the amount of moisture about 1in (2.5cm) below the surface of the compost. A moisture meter *can* be helpful, though in fairly coarse composts the readings are not always reliable. If you have decided that watering is necessary, then a thorough soaking must be given and the pot allowed to drain freely.

Growing on the Plants

Assuming that no second potting is required, the plant can be grown on in the same pot until the flowering season is over when it is encouraged to go into dormancy for the winter.

The success which the grower achieves with Tuberous begonias will depend considerably on the regular attention given to the plants during these important three or four months. There is no doubt whatsoever that the best results will come when the growing conditions have been as uniform as is possible during this time. If the plants are being grown for greenhouse decoration then attention to their needs every two or three days is probably sufficient except in the very hottest of weather. Large swings in the growing conditions will subject the plants to considerable physiological stress, which will always result in poor performance when it comes to flowering time. This stress must be reduced to as low a level as is possible by paying careful attention to the following cultural factors.

Atmospheric Humidity

The natural habitat of the parent species of this group of Tuberous begonias is high in the Andean mountains above a height of some 3,000m (*c.*10,000ft), where the plants are frequently bathed in mist. Not surprisingly the modern hybrids also appear to thrive (with the stems and foliage retaining their native suppleness) in a humid atmosphere.

A relative humidity of some 80 per cent is ideal up to the time that the flowering buds are allowed to develop. At this point the humidity can be reduced to around 50 per cent. This high humidity is fairly easily attained in large commercial glasshouses with a high apex, but not so in the smaller amateur greenhouse with a ridge height of 8–9ft (2.4–2.7m). In late spring and throughout the summer months when ventilators are wide open, a very short spell of sunshine can rapidly reduce the relative humidity even in a 30 × 10ft

(9 × 3m) greenhouse to well below 50 per cent. Investing in a dial hygrometer (moisture meter) is money well spent to check the humidity at all times. To maintain these high humidities it is necessary to inject water into the atmosphere, preferably as a 'mist', using a multi-headed fogging nozzle fitted to a mains water supply.

The advantage of using a fogging nozzle is that the water droplets produced are extremely small. Consequently not only do they wet surfaces much more efficiently, but they also remain suspended in the air far longer than those produced by ordinary sprayers. In bright, sunny weather this fogging may need to be done a number of times each day. In the absence of mains water the only alternative is saturating the floor of the greenhouse using water from a can, but this requires far more thought than a couple of gallons haphazardly sprinkled over the greenhouse area whenever you happen to remember.

As has been indicated above, when the time comes to allow the flowering buds to develop it is necessary to stop using a fogging nozzle in case the water droplets mark the backs of the dorsal petals. Experience to date has indicated that, so long as the water droplets are small enough, in the early stages of bud growth marking does not occur. Nonetheless it is not worth taking the risk. Under these circumstances humidity has to be maintained (though only at 50 per cent) by spreading water over the floor.

Temperature

Though the large and colourful blooms of the Tuberous begonias appear to be exotic and almost tropical in character, in fact they are essentially temperate, cool-growing subjects whose main enemy is high temperatures. The very fact that the parent species are found at such high altitudes means that they prefer the lower temperatures of around 60–65°F (16–18.5°C) for the best results. Indeed beyond either end of this range there is a strong tendency for growth to slow down, or even stop completely.

Once again it is not at all easy to keep the temperatures down in small greenhouses, particularly at midday under a full sun. One of the obvious advantages of commercial glasshouses is the very high ridge bar giving a large amount of headroom above the growing plants. For the amateur, where the normal ridge height is around 8ft (2.4m), plenty of ventilation is required. Extraction fans can help with the free movement of air, but of course this is going to result in a considerable reduction in atmospheric humidity.

If the greenhouse is a glass-to-ground type, or one built on a 12in

(30cm) high wall, then it is of considerable benefit to have low benches say 18in (45cm) from the floor. This has beneficial consequences: the humidity around the plants will be at the highest; the headroom above the plants will also be at a maximum; and the air close to the floor is the coolest in the greenhouse. The conflicting needs of ventilation and humidity means that a compromise is called for. One partial solution involves relying on ventilators (operated automatically) up to say 75–80°F (24–27°C), at which point a rising thermostat switches on an extraction fan.

In the early and late weeks of the growing season, as well as the occasional cool evening when temperatures can fall quite quickly, it is necessary to maintain at least 55°F (13°C) by supplementary heating. The expense involved in heating the whole greenhouse can be kept to a minimum in a normal season by starting tubers in mid-April, and confining the flowering period to a few weeks in August and very early September. Some growers line the inside of the greenhouse, or at least a portion of it, with bubble-cap plastic film which can significantly reduce heating costs.

When it comes to choosing the type of heating, it is really up to the individual. Paraffin and gas (mains as well as bottled) release large quantities of water into the atmosphere, and the heaters need to be properly adjusted if combustion products, deleterious to growth, are to be kept to a minimum. The extremely high humidities resulting from the production of water vapour is conducive to the appearance of fungal growths and moulds, and it must therefore be removed by adequate ventilation.

Though the needs for ventilation and greenhouse heating appear to conflict, the former is essential for plant health. Electrical heaters are useful because they can be considerably cheaper than some gas appliances, they are easily and accurately automated, they produce no noxious gases or vapours, and they can be run at very competitive rates. They do, however, require installation by a qualified electrician, and it is essential that the correct circuit-breaking facility is incorporated in the system.

Light and Shading

One of the aims and purposes of the American Begonia Society is to 'Stimulate and promote interest in begonias and other shade-loving plants'. This correctly infers that begonias prefer to avoid full sun, and that is certainly true of the Tuberhybridas. In fact low light conditions are equally to be avoided.

In their natural habitat the Tuberous begonias grow in fairly open areas, but on the shadier side of the mountains. The foliage of the modern hybrids is very soft and is readily scorched by direct sunlight, and so from April right through to September in Britain it is essential that the greenhouse is shaded. When scorching is extensive not only do the plants look dreadful, but the leaves are no longer able to carry out the photosynthesis required for healthy development. Growers who can site their greenhouses in the natural shading of tall trees are fortunate, though they have to be far enough away to receive plenty of filtered light. Of course if the trees are limes then each year the glass will be covered with sticky honeydew rapidly becoming almost black, and if the trees are chestnut then one has the problem of broken glass when the seeds fall. Trees too close to the greenhouse will reduce the light far too much and will 'draw' the plants, making them leggy.

The choice of shading is again in the hands of the grower. The choice is between the application of a green or white emulsion to the glass, or the use of shade cloth. Though the former method can be quite inexpensive it can also be quite difficult to remove excess emulsion from a cedar wood framed greenhouse, and this can detract from its appearance. There is also a product which, when applied to the glass, is opaque in dry weather but becomes transparent in wet weather. These types of shading are usually removed at the end of the season in September.

Various types of shade cloth, from extruded plastic netting to woven synthetic fibre, are also available. They can be purchased according to whether they allow 30, 50, or 60 per cent of the light (that is 70, 50, or 40 per cent shade value) through the cloth. The 50 per cent transmission quality is generally satisfactory for begonias, and is fastened to the outside of the structure or, alternatively, roller blinds can be made for outside or inside. Though in principle it is possible to use shade cloth only when the sun is shining and to remove it during dull spells, it is far more customary to leave the shading in position until September. There is now a new material on the market imported from Scandinavia, consisting of very thin strips of aluminium held together by woven synthetic fibre threads. This material can be made into a blind fitting horizontally above the plants and, when drawn, will reflect both the light and heat of the sun away from the greenhouse. As a bonus the blind can also act as a thermal blanket during the winter.

It is important to get the light level right for Tuberous begonias since it appears to have quite an effect on the depth of colour which is produced in the self-coloured varieties. Though one cannot prove the point scientifically, many believe that too high a light level can also cause colour run in some of the paler picotee varieties (for example 'Fred Martin'). Also, buds open more quickly in bright light and high temperatures giving rise to smaller flowers. The only guideline one can give is that when measured using a Weston Master V lightmeter (the type used in photography) the light value is best above 10 and below 13. Average values should be taken at the level of the plants and when the sun is full out at midday.

Maintaining the correct balance between atmospheric humidity, daytime temperatures and the light level is not possible, and compromise is essential. Frequently the changes in atmospheric conditions are such that we are unable to control the ultimate effect in the greenhouse – we must accept this situation and do all we can to minimize the worst conditions.

Watering

Perhaps the most difficult aspect of begonia cultivation is mastering when to water the plants. Certainly it is often said that more plants are ruined by over- than underwatering. This without any doubt was the position when loam-based composts were the normal growing medium. Today, if care is taken to ensure that the peat-based composts used have the correct air-filled porosity, it should be almost impossible to overwater the plants. Underwatering need be no problem either if the plants are examined on a regular basis.

As soon as a clay pot 'rings' it requires water or, in the case of a plastic pot, when the top 1in (2.5cm) of compost is dry. The plant must then be flooded and the pot is allowed to drain freely. Whether one is using mains or rainwater it is periodically worth while checking the pH (acidity or alkalinity) of the water going into, and that which drains from the pot using test papers obtainable from a chemist. If the water is occasionally found to be quite acidic (say lower than pH 6.0) a little lime added to the water will correct the pH to 6.5.

Watering must continue until after flowering when the amount given is reduced. This will be dealt with when discussing the end of season treatment.

Feeding

Almost every begonia grower has his or her own particular way of feeding begonias, and they will swear that 'no one can do it better'. I shall therefore do no more than indicate one method of successfully bringing Tuberous begonias to an acceptable level of flowering.

When grown in properly formulated loam-based composts it is extremely doubtful whether additional liquid feeding has any real value. When using peat-based formulations, however, the application of soluble feeds is necessary particularly when it is realized that the compost contains sufficient nutrient for only six weeks or so. It cannot be said too often that no 'miracle feed' or 'secret formulation' can convert a poor plant into a magnificent one. Correct feeding is but one of the aids to good cultivation, no more and no less important than a good compost, or the right watering, or a proper understanding of the required humidity and temperature. All of these factors are important in bringing a plant to its full potential. As with the other cultivation issues considered above, begonias do seem to prefer a small but consistent level of nutrients supplied throughout the growing season.

The nutrients required can be divided into three categories. Firstly is *micronutrients* – the elements which are required only in parts per million (for example: boron, chlorine, iron, molybdenum, copper, zinc and manganese). Their function in plant growth need not be considered further here except to say that good quality, loam-based composts always contained sufficient of these elements not to require further consideration. Peat-based composts, on the other hand, must be formulated so that these micronutrients are added in sufficient amounts. A convenient way to ensure that a home-made compost contains sufficient of these elements is to incorporate ½oz (14g) of Trace Element Frit 253A into every bushel of compost. Most commercial feeds, including the liquid ones as well as the base fertilizers, already contain the essential trace elements. It must be pointed out that, whilst the presence of these elements in trace amounts is beneficial, an excess of some might well be deleterious to growth even to the point of being toxic.

The second category contains the elements calcium, magnesium and sulphur. They are required in greater amounts than the micronutrients, but less than the macronutrients. Calcium of course is important to plant growth since, apart from its role in the formation of shoot tips, it assists in making nitrogen available to the growing plant. Magnesium is required for the production of chlorophyl which in turn is needed for photosynthesis.

The final category is macronutrients – the three elements nitrogen, phosphorous and potassium (known as the NPK elements) required in quantity by a growing plant. Most fertilizers and many liquid feeds carry an analysis of the percentages of these three elements available.

At this point one might briefly consider the roles played by the macronutrients in plant growth. For vigorous growth the plant needs a steady supply of available nitrogen throughout the whole season. Though it is possible for the plants to get small amounts of nitrogen from the atmosphere, the major source has to be in the form of applied fertilizer as ammonium, nitrate or urea. The first two are immediately available, whereas urea needs a slightly longer period to be converted into available nitrogen. Hoof and horn is an 'organic' form of nitrogen which is incorporated into composts where it requires the presence of bacteria and oxygen to break it down slowly into available nitrogen. Nitroform is an alternative source of nitrogen in composts where it breaks down more rapidly than hoof and horn. Nitrogen deficiency is seen first in the oldest leaves which tend to become yellow, accompanied by a general stunting in the overall growth.

Phosphorous is an essential element which converts the energy in sunlight into growth. It is provided in the form of organic fertilizers (such as hoof and horn or animal manures), or as inorganic phosphates (such as superphosphate) and the ammonium and potassium phosphates in liquid fertilizers. Phosphorous deficiency reveals itself in the development of brown areas on the leaves and petiole, and the appearance of dark blue/green leaves.

Potassium has a number of roles in the growth of plants, activating some of the enzymes needed for growth, helping to regulate the balance of salts in plant tissue, and assisting in helping to protect the plants from disease by thickening up cell walls. Potassium deficiency reveals itself in a number of ways – the leaf edges turn brown, spots appear on leaves surrounded by paler zones, leaves develop a metallic sheen, and leaves begin to roll inwards.

It must be stressed that the above signs are merely pointers to possible problems rather than diagnostic tests. Multiple deficiencies can greatly confuse the issue. No such deficiency should occur in home-produced composts when made according to the formulations given here, or on the packets of commercial base feeds.

Excessive acidity or alkalinity can also cause deficiencies in certain elements, even though those materials are present in abundance in the compost. In the vast majority of cases, however, as long as the pH is within the range 5.8–7.5, deficiency for these reasons is unlikely to occur. However, the availability of iron, which is one of the more important microelements so essential in the synthesis of chlorophyll, is severely restricted when the pH exceeds approximately 7.0. In purely practical terms, therefore, it is better to keep the pH of a compost between 5.8 and 7.0.

Excessive use of unbalanced fertilizer (such as very high potassium feeds) can also result in a deficiency in another element, for instance magnesium.

Whether one has chosen to use a commercial peat-based compost or prepared a home-made one using a purchased base fertilizer, there will be sufficient nutrient in the compost to satisfy the plant's basic needs for four to six weeks after potting. The root system will, however, have been seriously disturbed when the potting took place. It will therefore considerably help a young plant to recover if it is given a foliar feed each week for the following six weeks. There are many commercial liquid fertilizers which are suitable for such applications. Typical examples are Murphy's Foliar Feed, Maxicrop, Liquinure, Chempak No 2, etc.

The spray should be applied liberally to both sides of the leaves but not when the weather is dull. After about four or five weeks the root system should be growing well, and feeding can be switched from the foliage to the compost. A balanced fertilizer may be used, for example: Chempak No 3 or Liquinure applied once a week at half strength, or alternatively a higher potassium feed such as Phostrogen or Chempak No 4, again at half strength.

At the potting stage you must decide what kind of plant is required – multi- or a single-stemmed type. Other types of growth are possible but they are associated with exhibition work and will be dealt with in Chapter 11. For the time being we are considering only general greenhouse cultivation. In my opinion the best style of plant to cultivate is that which has a single, main stem with two side shoots since it is easy to handle, does not take up a large amount of bench space, and will produce flowers facing in one direction. That being the case all basal shoots in excess of the strongest one are removed when 2–3in (5–7.5cm) high and are used as cuttings, as described in Chapter 13.

Most large-flowered Tuberous begonias produce, in the leaf axils, buds or 'eyes' which grow on to become side shoots ultimately producing flowers. This, in general, is true for the first four leaves or so, beyond which the buds grow on to produce flowers only and no side shoots. So a plant with two side shoots can produce a most attractive flowering subject with up to nine blooms at any one time. There are, however, one or two varieties in which the tendency to produce flower buds in the lower leaf axils is greater than that of producing side shoots. If left to develop these lower flower buds would come to full bloom long before the main stem had grown sufficiently. Consequently these varieties do not always make attractive small pot plants. Two such varieties are 'Peach Melba' and 'Bernat Klein', though there are others.

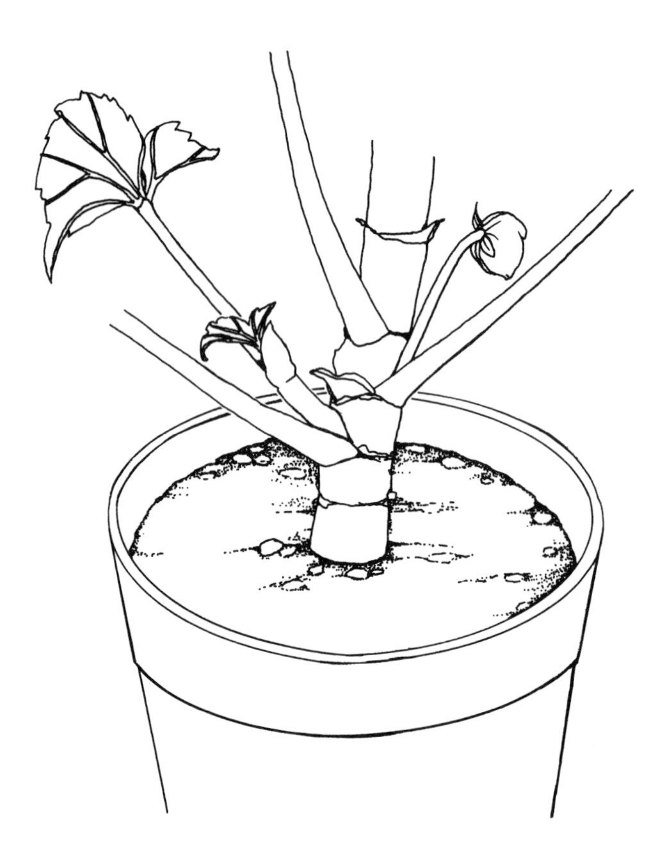

This illustrates the difference between a side shoot and a flower growth.

It should not be necessary to grow in pots greater than 8in (20cm) in diameter, and probably 7in (18cm) would be, in most cases, quite suitable. Certainly tubers of say two to four years old could be accommodated in the smaller size pot.

As the plant develops, the main stem is loosely secured to the stake and all buds are removed until the stem is carrying about five or six leaves. At this stage all buds of about the same size on the main stem and the side shoots are left on the plant to develop into blooms. Any buds much smaller than these are also retained for further flower production. If the largest buds left on the plant measure some 1⅛in (3cm) at the widest point they will take approximately 5–6 weeks to develop into fully opened blooms.

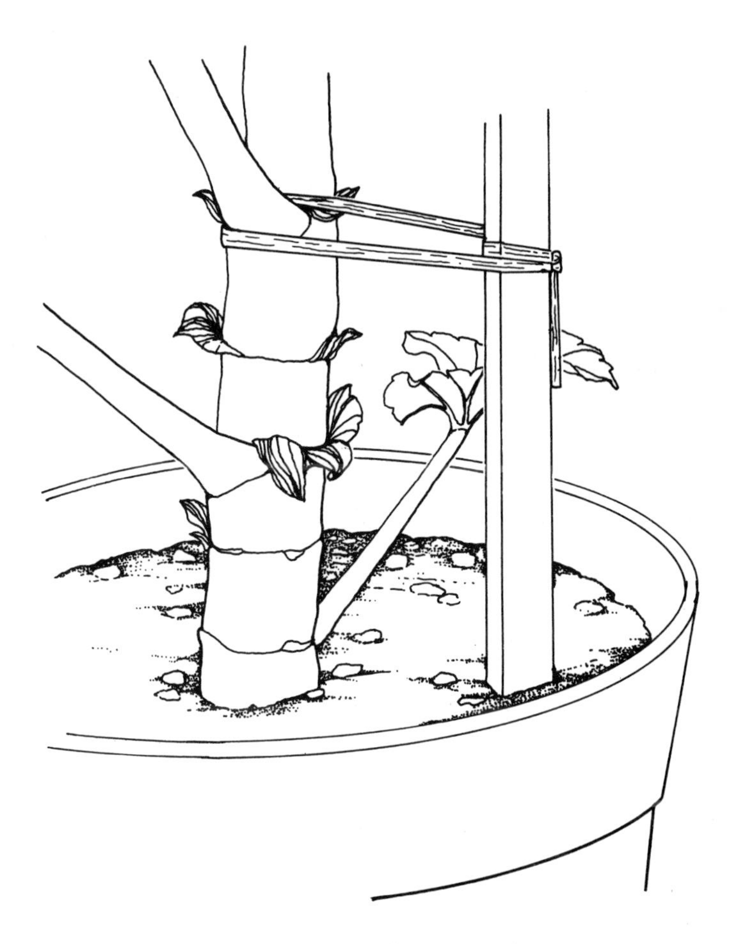

Staking the growing plant. A loose tie of raffia, polypropylene or fillis string is used to prevent excessive movement of the growing plant.

Slightly larger buds will take correspondingly less time, and smaller ones longer.

As they increase in size it will be noted that the centre male bud is flanked by two others often, but not always, female. These two flanking buds must be pinched out as soon as possible to enable all the growth to be concentrated into the one central male bloom. As they become larger it might be sensible to support the buds by placing bloom supports under the neck of the flower stem. The spring-adjusted extending type, with a plastic stirrup, is the easiest one to handle and gives close control on the height and position of the bloom. At about the time that the buds are allowed to develop the plant can be top dressed with a 1in (2.5cm) layer of compost identical to the one used for potting.

As soon as the flowers are past their best they should be removed with the next batch of buds being allowed to bloom. It is best, at this stage, to 'stop' the plant by pinching out the growing points so that after this second flush of flower no further blooms can form. In any case the size of flowers will now begin to decrease quite quickly, and it is hardly worth allowing them to develop.

GARDEN CULTIVATION

Tubers intended for outdoor use need not have shoots removed, and all should be allowed to develop.

The planting site is initially prepared by extensive digging, and ensuring that it is well drained. On a very wet site this might require removing the top 12in (30cm) of soil, digging coarse gravel into the subsoil, and replacing the topsoil having first enriched it in moisture-retaining humus – either well-rotted compost, peat, or well-rotted farmyard manure. The site should be selected so that the begonias will ultimately be shaded from direct sun either by a hedge or by taller plants in the garden. Though they are not plants which grow at all well in dark areas, they do scorch extremely quickly when exposed to the midday sun.

Plants started in the greenhouse are planted out about 14in (35cm) apart in early June, or as soon as all danger of ground frost has gone. Alternatively, tubers showing growth shoots can be placed directly into the ground in May as long as they are planted well below the soil surface. All early buds should be removed until the plants are growing strongly – a light sprinkling of granular fertilizer around the plants will help to sustain them during their heavy flowering period. There is no need to remove the female

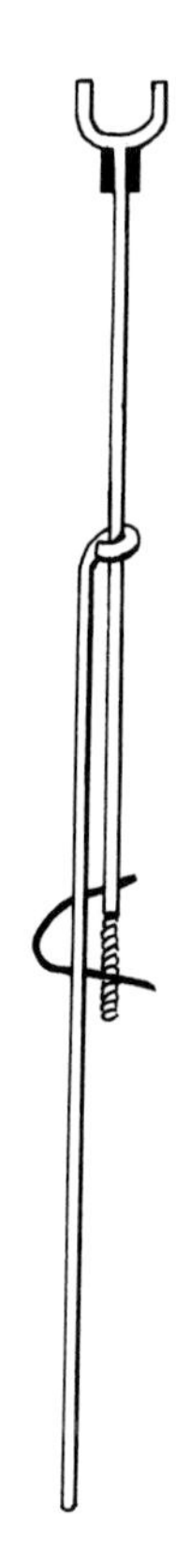

A much improved bloom support available from the National Begonia Society.

buds from outdoor begonias since they help to enhance the colourful show of bloom.

When planting out note that where there are only one or two main stems to a plant, they should be so placed that the flowers can easily be seen. Also, since begonias have succulent but brittle stems, and therefore suffer considerably from wind damage in the open garden, they should be fastened to stakes.

HARVESTING TUBERS

As October approaches the 'stopped' greenhouse plants will be producing no new flowers, and the time is approaching when they will want to become dormant. Watering will now have to be considerably reduced, though the plants must not be allowed to become dry – a watering with a small amount of sulphate of potash (¼ teaspoon per gl – 4.5l) will help to harden or ripen the tuber. At this stage the top 6in (15cm) of growth can be removed and the pots stood pot deep on the benches. As much ventilation as possible is given to reduce the likelihood of stem rot attacking the plants, and daily inspection is essential to remove fallen leaves. The greenhouse temperature is kept as low as possible, but not below 45°F (7.5°C).

Slowly the leaves will yellow and fall away and, as this happens, the main stem must be reduced gradually, leaving the final section to fall naturally. If it is not possible to examine the state of the plants on a daily basis then you can stack the pots on their sides so that, as the leaves and stems fall, they do not drop on to the compost surface where they can lead to rot in the lower stem and tuber.

It must be said that this protracted period of ripening the tubers is the time when so many growers lose their stock through rotting, either from lack of attention to hygiene or, alternatively, trying to induce dormancy too quickly. Admittedly it is not a very exciting time in the cycle of begonia cultivation, but it is one which is vital to the continuing good health of the tuber. The period of dormancy must be allowed to develop quite naturally if the tubers are to be kept in good heart through the winter months.

Tubers grown in the garden are treated somewhat differently, being left in their flowering positions until the first frost of the late autumn. When the tops have been blackened by the first light frost, the stems are cut down to about 6in (15cm) and the tubers lifted complete with a ball of soil. These labelled plants are placed in a box in a dry, cool place and allowed to stand until the soil falls away and the residual stems are shed.

At this stage all tubers, whether cultivated in the greenhouse or in the garden, are thoroughly cleaned using a fairly stiff nail-brush and all the compost and the majority of the root system are removed, though care must be taken not to damage the outer skin of the tuber. Considerable care is required when brushing off any residual compost, especially when the medium is wet since the outer skin of the tuber is so easily damaged under these conditions. A thorough examination for any sign of damage, either from disease or pest, is carried out. Any rot is ruthlessly cut away and the wound dusted with a mixture of sulphur and Benlate.

The correct labels are now attached by rubber bands and the tubers are stored in a cool but dry place until the following year.

A temperature of 40–45°F (4.5–7.5°C) is ideal for winter storage. Some growers prefer to place every tuber in a paper (not plastic) bag, some keep them in wooden boxes, and others store them dry in polystyrene boxes properly insulated from rapid fluctuations in temperature. All tubers should be thoroughly examined for signs of rot every four weeks through the winter.

NAMED VARIETIES

The varieties below, classified according to colour, are just a few of those available today, some raised by amateurs and others by the specialist commercial nurseries. Each of these varieties can be grown fairly easily according to the principles described above and will readily produce a most attractive single-stemmed plant for the cool greenhouse.

White or Cream

'Avalanche'
One of the best all-round white begonias. The large white blooms have a rather ragged appearance due to the slightly wavy petals.

'Bernat Klein'
A beautiful white variety which, though robust, does not produce many side shoots.

'Billie Langdon'
A very free-flowering variety with quite large pure white flowers. The blooms have a classic shape with wide, overlapping petals.

'Diana Wynyard'
One of the older varieties, fairly dwarf growing. Prolific in producing side shoots and flowers late in the season. The pure white flowers are of great depth, but would benefit from more petals.

'Full Moon'
Very large blooms of classic shape with a rich, creamy colour. The plant is a vigorous grower producing plenty of side shoots.

'Icicle'
An Australian variety where the white blooms have a greenish tinge to the centre.

'Snowbird'
Large, deep, pure white flowers on a very erect plant. The blooms quickly assume a 'cup and saucer' shape as the back petals fold back.

Yellow

'Festiva'
Quite an old yellow-flowering variety where the blooms are of intermediate size with rather a hard, chrome yellow colour.

'Goldilocks'
A new (1990) variety with deep, golden yellow, slightly serrated petals.

'Joburg'
A vigorous growing variety with golden yellow flowers of true rosebud shape. This is an excellent amateur hybrid.

'Lillian Thornton'
A very pale, primrose yellow bloom in which there is a strong tendency for the pink pigment to show through the back petals.

'Majesty'
Deeper primrose yellow blooms are freely produced. The complete flower has a somewhat square look about it. Very susceptible to attacks of mildew.

'Midas'
A fairly compact plant with golden yellow blooms against a very attractive dark-green foliage. Really good, yellow begonias are few and far between, and tend to be measured against this variety.

'Primrose'
Very pale yellow blooms which are slightly frilled. Extremely free-flowering – needs to have the number of blooms reduced to increase the size of the remaining flowers.

Orange

'City of Ballaarat'
Quite a stunning variety. The large, brilliant, orange blooms have broad and very slightly wavy petals and a perfect rosebud centre.

'Hawaii'
A bright orange flower, of huge size, with large, deckle-edged petals. The orange colour pales slightly towards the centre of the bloom.

'Margaret'
An amateur-raised variety with mid-orange flowers with a trace of bicolour. Occasionally this variety has a pronounced tendency to produce many undersized blooms.

'Orange Sensation'
A brilliant clear orange bloom of good size and form. Smooth overlapping petals. An amateur hybrid.

'Zoe Colledge'
Similar to 'City of Ballaarat', though a slightly paler orange. The colour is highlighted against the paler green foliage.

Apricot/Peach

'Apricot Delight'
Very large flowers of a pale apricot shade. The edges of the petals are serrated. A very robust variety and extremely free-flowering.

'Flo' Willsmore'
An Australian variety with delicate, apricot-coloured blooms. The petals are deeply serrated giving the appearance of being almost fimbriated.

'Sea Coral'
A new (1990) variety with broad petals and a rosebud centre. The bloom colour is coral with a hint of peach. Freely produces side shoots.

'Suzanne Redmayne'
An amateur-raised variety with very great potential. Rather a tall grower it can produce massive blooms which also have great depth. The blooms have a distinct apricot colour with very heavy rosebud centres.

'Tahiti'
For most growers this is a 'banker'. Since its introduction it has perhaps taken more top show awards than any other variety. The

huge coral apricot blooms consist of broad petals which can be more or less frilled. If the plant is cultivated in too low light conditions the bloom centres can become almost white.

Red

'Allan Langdon'
A brilliant crimson begonia with a touch of purple in the pigment. The variety is very free-flowering and vigorous.

'Goliath'
A new (1990) variety which has enormous tomato ketchup coloured blooms. The broad petals are slightly deckle-edged and the flowers are almost perfect in shape.

'Linda Jackson'
An amateur-raised begonia, and possibly the best red for many years. The shade is not unlike that of 'Red Admiral' but the blooms are longer lasting and the plant is altogether more vigorous.

'Red Admiral'
Bright, crimson-red flowers but, like most others in this range, the velvety textured petals mark extremely easily. The variety is a strong grower though not a prolific producer of side shoots. The dark green leaves make an attractive backdrop to the red flowers.

'Royalty'
A variety introduced many years ago, but still on sale. The blooms, though not very large, are classic rosebud shape. The rich crimson petals are like luxurious velvet in texture, though unfortunately they have the tendency to mark very easily. The foliage is a mid-green, and the contrast between the blooms and leaves is most attractive.

'Ruby Wedding'
Deep crimson, reminiscent of 'Royalty', though the blooms are larger and of better form. This is another amateur hybrid.

'Scarlet O'Hara'
The vivid, scarlet-red flowers can be very large but the bloom will suffer from a coarse appearance. The strong stems make this a big improvement on the earlier variety 'Guardsman'.

'Sultan'
Mid-crimson red blooms with a soft velvety texture. The long-lasting flowers are not particularly large, but of classic rosebud form.

'Tom Brownlee'
A very recent amateur hybrid and wholly spectacular. It can produce huge blooms in a most vibrant shade of red and with great depth. Very broad overlapping petals, and a classic form.

'Zulu'
Not a particularly large-flowered variety, but once again the blooms are perfect in shape with a crimson red even deeper in shade than 'Sultan'.

Bicolours/Picotees

It is not always clear whether certain varieties are bicolours or picotees, and this is particularly true where the picotee edge is very broad and the colour tends to spread into the whole petal.

'Beverly B'
An amateur-raised hybrid not too dissimilar to the above.

'Blushing Bride'
An Australian variety with medium-size blooms. The heavily ruffled petals are white and tipped with a fine red edge.

'Can-Can'
A tall variety with a spectacular, yellow ground, red-edged bloom and slightly frilled. In the wrong light conditions the yellow colour fades badly, changing the whole character of the variety.

'Dorothy White'
Another and recently introduced bicolour where the basic petal colour is yellow but overlaid with red. This is a vigorous grower and very floriferous – produces lots of side shoots.

'Fairylight'
A white ground picotee with broad, flat petals with a fine scarlet red edge. Very free-flowering and sufficient side shoots to make a well-balanced plant.

'Fred Martin'
Named after the late Secretary of the British National Begonia Society this is a wonderful variety and, at its best, is one of the finest varieties ever raised. The plant habit is extremely sturdy and compact. The large flowers, of perfect shape and form, are cream with a fine pink edge. A fine picotee which should be in every collection.

'Geisha Girl'
A new picotee with broad white petals and a very pronounced, substantial, red edge.

'Jean Blair'
An old variety but still widely grown and currently available. The flowers, which are not large, are of a rich, yellow ground with a distinct red edge and slightly frilled. There is a tendency for the red edge to spread into the bulk of the petal, especially in a very hot season.

'Jessie Cruickshank'
A most attractive white ground picotee with a distinct red edge to the frilled petals. A most successful introduction by an amateur grower.

'Peach Melba'
A lovely bicolour introduced in 1973 but still extremely popular today. The slightly wavy petals are a pale apricot shade overlaid with the softest orange. The precise depth of colour is very much dependent upon the light intensity.

Pink

This is one colour range where the choice of variety is very large indeed. Here we give only a small selection as illustration.

'Falstaff'
Probably one of the finest begonias – a very compact grower producing huge, deep blooms in a deep rose-pink colour. Occasionally there is a tendency for the centre of the blooms to be almost white.

'Gypsy'
Another deep-pink variety raised by an amateur.

'Jenny Barclay'
This very robust variety, raised by an amateur, produces very large blooms which are frilled. The eye-catching deep-pink blooms have an almost perfect form.

'Judy Langdon'
Large, pale, salmon-pink flowers produced in profusion on a most vigorous plant. The large, smooth petals have prominent veining which adds character to the variety.

'Krakatoa'
An amateur-raised, floriferous variety. The blooms, which are lightly frilled, are of a reddish-pink shade and are often mistaken for a red begonia.

'Roy Hartley'
One of the all-time begonia greats. The very large, slightly ruffled blooms are a soft shade of pink tinged with a salmon shade. The precise colour is highly dependant upon the intensity of the light and tends to be deeper under lower light levels.

'Sugar Candy'
The large, clear pink blooms are produced earlier in the season than on many other varieties.

There are many additional varieties available from both specialist nurseries and amateur hybridists. It is, however, unfortunately true that not all named varieties lend themselves to cultivation as pot plants.

4
PENDULA AND CASCADES

HISTORY AND DEVELOPMENT

The history of Tuberous begonias, which includes Pendula and Cascade types, is not very well documented. There is little doubt that they derive their long slender stems from the species *B. boliviensis*, and indeed one of the very early examples of this group 'B. Lloydii' also was characterized by the species' long, narrow, drooping flowers.

For many years the name 'B. Lloydii' was synonymous with Pendula begonias and, until approximately five years ago, plants were still being sold under this name. They had the same single, long, narrow-petalled flowers as the very early examples. Just over 100 years ago there appeared a hybrid known as 'Doctor Moore' (probably a mutant of *B. boliviensis*) which had the ability to convey semi-double characteristics rather easily to its progeny. This led to the so-called 'Boucher' strain of Pendula begonias, of which one of the most significant was the variety 'B. Chrysanthemiflora', a pendulous variety with blooms resembling a chrysanthemum. Since the early 1900s development of the Pendula types leant towards plants with small double- or semi-double flowers. In England the firm of Blackmore & Langdon (presumably developing the 'Boucher' strain) produced 'Mrs. Bilkey', an orange cultivar still with rather pointed petals. This variety was still for sale in the 1970s.

Much of the progress since the first decade of the 1900s had been the development of the small, double-flowered Pendulous types with an extended colour range. This involved crossing the early varieties with an unnamed, large-flowered Tuberous double, and back-crossing on to *B. boliviensis*. This led to the small-flowered Pendula begonias which had somewhat narrow petals and frequently semi-double flowers. The foliage was also very distinctive in that the leaves were long and narrow, and occasionally somewhat serrated at the margins. This of course is very reminiscent of the parent species.

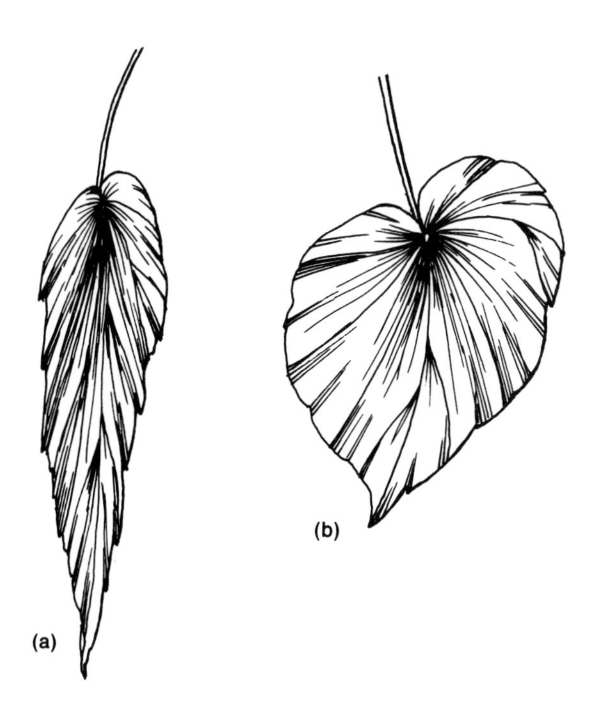

Leaf shapes of small- and large-flowered Pendula begonias: (a) the long, narrow, slightly serrated leaf shape reminiscent of B. boliviensis; *(b) the much rounder leaf shape of the modern Cascade begonias.*

As far as can be ascertained these small-flowered Pendulas were all diploids, and as such were fertile. Since the original species used has red flowers (and no genes for yellow shades), the fact that some of the Boucher strains were reddish golden (for example 'Louis Boucher') meant an unrecorded begonia must have been involved in the early work.

Apart from small improvements to bloom form, and an extension of the colour range, very little further development took place until the middle 1940s when the American firm of Vetterle & Reinelt undertook an intensive hybridization programme in which they crossed the then Pendulous begonias with selected Tuberous doubles, which already possessed long drooping flower stalks and blooms with rosebud centres or highly ruffled petals. The results were the Cascades of today, plants which have large and almost completely double flowers on pendulous stems which can reach 3ft (90cm) in length, carrying much larger leaves. Though it is incorrect to suggest that this type of Pendula begonia should have a separate grouping from the above, to mark the obvious differences they are called the large-flowered Pendula begonias, or Cascades. These Pendulas are tetraploid and far less fertile than their small-flowered relations.

The other development which has taken place is the breeding of a slight perfume into one or two varieties which were named 'Yellow Sweetie' and 'Orange Sweetie', and became available in 1947. With regard to fragrance in the hybrid Tuberous begonias it must be said that individuals differ widely in their ability to detect any scent at all. It is also true that some people refer to it as a smell rather than a fragrance, and the word 'cats' is not infrequently used to identify it! In 1990 two new fragrant varieties were made available in America, 'B. Sweet Dianne' and 'B. Golden Anniversary', both raised by Howard Siebold but released under different names. Again the fragrance – and not, I hasten to add, that of cats – is a little elusive and depends on the atmospheric conditions and time of day.

Today there are a number of Cascade begonias available in red, orange, apricot, yellow and white, and in red-edged white picotee. The flower form is much improved on that of a few years ago though there is still some way to go before it approaches that of the large-flowered Tuberous doubles. I suppose the real question is whether the form can be further improved without sacrificing either the quantity of flower or the pendulous, branching habit.

As with the large-flowered doubles the named varieties represent the most reliable value for money. Unnamed varieties in separate colours are available from the specialist begonia nurseries, and they all have double flowers which are large for Pendulas. Unnamed Pendula begonias are also imported from Europe and many, though quite attractive, are the narrow, long-petalled type. Pendula seed can also be purchased, but once again many of the plants obtained in this way yield the narrow-petalled flowers. Seed purchased from the specialist begonia nurseries is most likely to give the large-flowered types.

CULTIVATION

The cultivation of Pendula or Cascade begonias is similar to that for the large-flowered Tuberous doubles, except that in these cases no stems are removed from the plant. The greater the number of flowering stems the more attractive will be the end product. There is some advantage to be gained from starting the tubers into growth as early as possible, for example January, so that the plant has as long a growing season as possible thus giving the stems ample opportunity to develop. The tubers should be started into growth using bottom heat of 70°F (21°C), and in the same compost as used for their larger cousins.

There is much to be said for reducing the flowers to an absolute minimum during the first year, thus encouraging the tuber to build up its reserves – a two-year-old tuber will give much more satisfactory results. Unlike the large-flowered Tuberous doubles it is better to start Pendula begonias in a pot rather than a tray. This reduces the amount of root damage when it becomes necessary to move on the plants. For an average two-year-old tuber a 3–3½in (7.5–9cm) pot should be adequate, whilst older tubers might need to go into a 4in (10cm) pot. After about six weeks in the pots the plants should be knocked out to check the development of the root system. If it is going well then this is the time to prepare the baskets in which the plants will flower.

A 12in (30cm) diameter basket will need up to three plants from the small, two- to three-year-old tubers, though two or even one of the older and larger tubers should be adequate. The basket is lined with either live sphagnum moss (or florist's moss) or alternatively (but not nearly as attractively) one of the commercial basket liners. A layer of coarse peat is placed at the bottom of the basket to provide drainage. A small amount of the peat-based compost (as described in Chapter 3) is then placed on top of the peat, and three empty pots, identical to the ones in which the plants are growing, are sited symmetrically around the inside of the basket and angled towards the rim. More compost is then added and gently firmed around the empty pots, and finished off by forming a slight depression in the centre of the basket. The compost is now watered by gentle immersion in a bucket of water and allowed to drain thoroughly (this can be done by standing the basket on a bucket). When draining is over, the empty pots are gently removed and replaced by the plants which have been knocked out of their containers. A gentle firming with the fingers completes the task of planting up the basket.

The basket, standing on the bucket, is next placed in the greenhouse at 50–60°F (10–16°C) in good light, but not direct sunlight. The compost is watered when necessary and given an occasional immersion to ensure the compost is thoroughly soaked.

A number of authors have suggested that it is better to pinch out growing points early in the growing period to encourage the plant to branch. However, with contemporary hybrids this should not be necessary since the propensity for branching is an important factor in their breeding and selection. Normally, the first four or five axillary buds on each stem are ones which produce side shoots, whereas the subsequent buds are flower producers. This is, of course, why the flowers on Pendula begonias tend to congregate at the ends of the trailing stems. Pinching out will simply remove these prospective flower buds.

When the stems are long enough to trail over the side of the basket it can be hung in the apex of the greenhouse. It is worth while visualizing what the basket will look like when it is in full flower, and estimating the eventual weight which will have to be supported. From now on the basket must be kept watered and fed frequently with a fertilizer whose NPK rating is approximately 33:10:10, the high element of nitrogen encouraging rapid growth of the stems. All the buds should now be removed to encourage the plant growth.

Some of the basket begonias are susceptible to powdery mildew attacks, and therefore a preventative spraying with Nimrod-T, or a fungicide containing Dinocap, will help keep the plant free of infection. Since the basket will probably be close to the glass considerable care must be taken to ensure that foliage scorching does not occur – on the other hand a heavy degree of shading will result in weak, drawn growth. When rapid growth is under way and the plants have acclimatized to their new environment the buds may be left on the plant to develop. The whole flower cluster is left on the plant. No removal of the flanking buds is required since the beauty of the Pendula begonias depends on as much flower colour as possible, and not on flower form or the size of the male bloom. Today's modern Cascades do not produce the stem lengths of the Pendulas of 30 years ago when it was necessary, in the show schedules, to specify that a basket on display had to be 5ft (1.5m) above the staging. The present-day varieties produce trailing stems of perhaps 30in (76cm) in length, though the flowers are much larger and the whole effect is very attractive. The nature of the growth is such that a mass of flower is produced towards the ends of the main stems, and the multitude of side shoots give the effect of a solid collar of colour about 12in (30cm) deep.

VARIETIES

Some of the earlier varieties which are still grown today, but which cannot be purchased from the nurseries are:

'Mrs. Bilkey': Salmon-orange.
'Roberta': Deep scarlet.
'Dawn': Buff yellow.
'Bettina': Large flowers of salmon-pink.
'Golden Shower': Peach colour with camellia-like flowers.

Two which are still available for purchase are:

'Yellow Sweetie': Pale yellow in colour with a delicate sweet scent.
'Lou Anne': Pale rose-pink.

Of the Cascade series several have been deleted from the catalogues but may still be obtainable through colleagues, these are:

'Red Cascade': Deep scarlet.
'Rose Cascade': Rose-pink.
'Apricot Cascade': Very pale orange.
'Picotee Cascade': White flowers with palest pink edge.
'Scarlet Cascade': Scarlet blooms with dark-green foliage.

The Cascades available today through the nurseries are:

'Bridal Cascade': Red-edged picotee.
'Crimson Cascade': Rich, deep, prolific red.
'Gold Cascade': Chrome yellow.
'Orange Cascade': Bright orange blooms.
'Pink Cascade': Very pale pink.

It would be quite wrong to conclude this chapter on Pendula and Cascade begonias without including one of the most striking examples of a plant with pendulous habit, though it is not a hybrid. This is of course *B. sutherlandii* a species introduced from Africa in 1863. This Tuberous begonia has slender 20in (50cm) tall stems with attractive pale-green leaves and a multitude of small, single, orange flowers. Because of the slender nature of the main stems *B. sutherlandii* is well suited for growing in a basket. It is very susceptible to attacks of mildew and therefore needs regular spraying with a fungicide. The plant produces small bulbils in the leaf axils in late summer which may be collected, stored over the winter, and planted as seeds in the following spring.

B. sutherlandii, like all Tuberous begonias, can be propagated from stem or basal cuttings though it is much more satisfactory to use the bulbil method. A hybrid from *B. sutherlandii*, named Begonia 'Pink Parasol', has been raised by Robert Hamm in America. It is Non-tuberous and, unlike the parent, has no period of dormancy. It has small, deeply cut leaves and five-petalled pink flowers, and is equally suitable for basket cultivation.

5
MULTIFLORAS, NON-STOPS, AND CLIPS

These Tuberous begonias are small-flowered types with very compact, bushy growth habits. Though they can be grown just like the large-flowered Tuberous doubles in a cool greenhouse, their relatively poor flower form and bushy growth make them preferable as garden subjects where their multi-blooms can be a considerable asset. Some of them, particularly the single-flowered Multifloras, are very decorative as houseplants since they do not drop their flowers quite as readily as the larger-flowered kind.

HISTORY

The Multiflora types were the first to be developed in this group and their origins go back to the 1870s with the release of hybrids developed from the species *B. davisii*. The characteristics of this species, including a low bushy habit, flowers held high above the foliage, and a free-flowering nature, were the very desirable ones handed on to the progeny. The other species involved in these early crosses were *B. pearcei* and *B. veitchii*, the former contributing its golden yellow characteristics thus making possible a wider colour range in the flowers ranging from red, through copper, to yellow, as well as its most attractive foliage of rich, dark, velvety green with lighter veins. The latter species conferred much rounder flowers on its progeny, with stiffer flower stems holding the blooms above the foliage.

As far as can be ascertained the very earliest hybrid of this type was obtained by Veitch and named 'Mrs. Arthur Potts' in 1878. Other hybrids followed quickly, with flower colours still in the pink/red range. About the same time some development was continuing in Germany where perhaps one of the most successful *B. davisii* crosses led to 'Graf Zeppelin', a red double-flowered cultivar which was still available until a few years ago.

From around 1890 much of the development occurred in France with Louis Urbain introducing *B. pearcei* into the *B. davisii* crosses. In this period the cultivars 'Helen Harmes' and 'Flamboyant' were produced – the former a double-yellow, and the latter a single-red, both still being available today. After 1918 much of the development switched to Belgium and some of the varieties produced, such as 'Jewel of Ghent', 'Mme. Richard Gallè', and 'Switzerland', are still very popular as outdoor flowering plants.

The varieties mentioned above are merely those which have retained a degree of popularity over the years, but they represent a small fraction of the hybrids which were produced – one list alone contains some 120 named varieties once available.

As has been mentioned some of the Multiflora begonias grown are single-flowered types, but even the double-flowered varieties do not have the perfection of flower form of the large-flowered Tuberous doubles. Even these so-called doubles are not fully double, which tends to lessen their attraction. There is a fairly wide range of colours available, for instance red, yellow, salmon, apricot, which stand up extremely well to bright sunlight, though perhaps not quite so well as some of the Semperflorens. Given the right conditions they can be very floriferous and almost ideal as bedding plants.

The only problem is that they are not grown from seed but need to be propagated vegetatively. This is a considerable drawback which makes the cost of using them as bedding plants quite high. However, they are reasonably attractive as edging or patio plants where their masses of brightly coloured flowers contrast with the small, vivid, green leaves. Their use individually as house plants also makes them worthy of discussion.

As we have noted the drawback of this group was that propagation was vegetative and not through seed production. About the time of the First World War attempts were made to develop a strain of these small, bedding-type begonias which could be propagated from seed. One report claims that, from a cross of a Tuberous hybrid with a Semperflorens begonia, an F1 tuberous generation was obtained. Subsequent crossing with one of the Multiflora group led to a new race of begonias which were very free-flowering dwarf plants, but which could be propagated from seed. These were named Multiflora maxima, or sometimes Multiflora grandiflora, but now are simply Begonia maxima.

There is still some confusion today because the begonias 'Switzerland' and 'Masquerade' are sold as Multifloras, when in reality they should be classified as Maximas. This confusion probably arises because there is an alternative background to the development of the Maxima group, which is different from that described. According to this theory the group was produced in Germany during the Second World War by crossing the large-flowered Tuberous doubles with selected members of the Multiflora group, which indeed is the origin of the begonias 'Switzerland' and the picotee 'Masquerade'.

These two lines of development are undoubtedly correct, though whether the products are identical is another matter. Certainly the plants of the Maxima group are slightly taller than the Multifloras, the flowers are larger – with a diameter of 2–3in (5–7.5cm), they are fully double, and are held well above the foliage. The leaves of this group are also larger than those of the Multifloras, and altogether they give the appearance of being somewhat scaled-down versions of the large, flowered, double-begonias, though without their excellent form.

In the last three decades further breeding both in Europe and America has continued, with the Maxima group in developing the Non-stop and the Clips, again retaining the compact habit with many small (that is, up to 3in – 7.5cm) blooms. One plant of a Clip can produce as many as 30 flowers. The Clips appear to be somewhat more vigorous than the Non-stops, but both make ideal garden plants fairly resistant to changes in the weather. In the 1970s the nursery of Ernst Benary in Germany had on sale named varieties of Non-stops – for instance 'Non-stop Apricot', 'Non-stop Gold', 'Non-stop Scarlet', and 'Non-stop Salmon' – but today these have all but disappeared and now the Non-stops and Clips are grown as F1 hybrids from widely available seed.

CULTIVATION

As we have said the Non-stops and Clips are raised from seed which is planted as early as possible in the season, say December or January. Though, as we have observed, this type of begonia is not usually thought of as a greenhouse plant, nevertheless it must be grown on exactly like any other tuberous begonia in a warm greenhouse. When the seedlings are large enough for transplanting they are transferred to trays subdivided into pots 3¼in × 2¾in (8 × 7cm), one plant per pot. Any early buds can be removed at this stage, and as soon as all chance of frost has disappeared the plants can be planted out in a prepared site as described for the large-flowered Tuberous types.

In the first year it is likely that these will be only one stem, and this should be allowed to flower at will leaving the female flowers on the plant. Note should be taken of those plants which you may wish to dispose of, for example the odd one which is either single or not fully double. By the end of September, or the onset of cold weather, the top 6in (15cm) of the plants can be removed and each one lifted, complete with a ball of soil. If kept in a cool, dry place the soil, and the remaining growth, will eventually fall away leaving a small tuber. These tubers should be kept through the winter in a box of *very slightly* moist peat and in a cool but frost-free place.

In February of the following season these small tubers can be started into growth with a degree of bottom heat, just like their larger cousins as described in Chapter 5. As each year goes by the tubers should produce a greater number of shoots, thus providing an ever-increasing mass of flower.

At a slightly increased cost the members of this group can also be grown from tubers purchased from most seedsmen, which are sold in individual colours or mixed. The method of cultivating, harvesting and storing the tubers is as described above.

It is still possible to purchase a few named varieties, though in some instances they are not widely available:

Multiflora

'Helene Harmes': Canary yellow, semi-double.
'Mme. Richard Gallè': Salmon-orange, semi-double.
'Gents Jewel': Salmon, semi-double.
'Le Flamboyant': Cherry red, single.

Multiflora Maxima

'Flamboyant': Cherry red, double.
'Switzerland': Dark red, double.

Non-stops

'Non-stop Series': In apricot, gold, orange, pink, salmon, scarlet.

6
OTHER TUBEROUS BEGONIAS

With the developments in Tuberhybrida over the past 100 years or so, a number of separate groups have come and gone, each with its own specific characteristics. Such groups as the Crispa, Cristata, Narcissiflora, and Bertinii, etc., have for a while enjoyed some popularity and then all but disappeared without trace. The reasons for this are difficult to ascertain, but certainly it is a situation which must be regretted. Today there is an overwhelming interest in Britain, almost to the exclusion of any other Tuberous types, of the cultivation of the named, large-flowered doubles. The Cascades have a reasonable following, and the outdoor growing of Multifloras and Non-stops, already quite considerable, is on the increase.

However, all is not lost since there are one or two other Tuberous begonias which are available and cultivated, albeit on a small scale. This is a great pity since each of them has a special attraction in its own right, quite distinct from any association they might have with their large-flowered relations. Here we shall mention briefly the Fimbriata, Crispa marginata and Marmorata types.

MARMORATA BEGONIAS

The earliest reference to a double-flowered hybrid, in which the flower was blotched or marbled with white, goes back to around 1900, though a single-flowered hybrid with a similar marbled flower had been shown in France some five years earlier. It was to this single-flowered hybrid that the name Marmorata was given, but since this cultivar no longer exists then no confusion with the double-flowered hybrids of the same name is possible.

In the first decade of the 1900s extensive work in France and Belgium extended the range of varieties available to pink, orange, scarlet and dark-red flowers, all marbled with white. J. Haegeman, in his book *Tuberous Begonias* (1979), records that they are all now extinct with perhaps the exception of one cultivar with red and

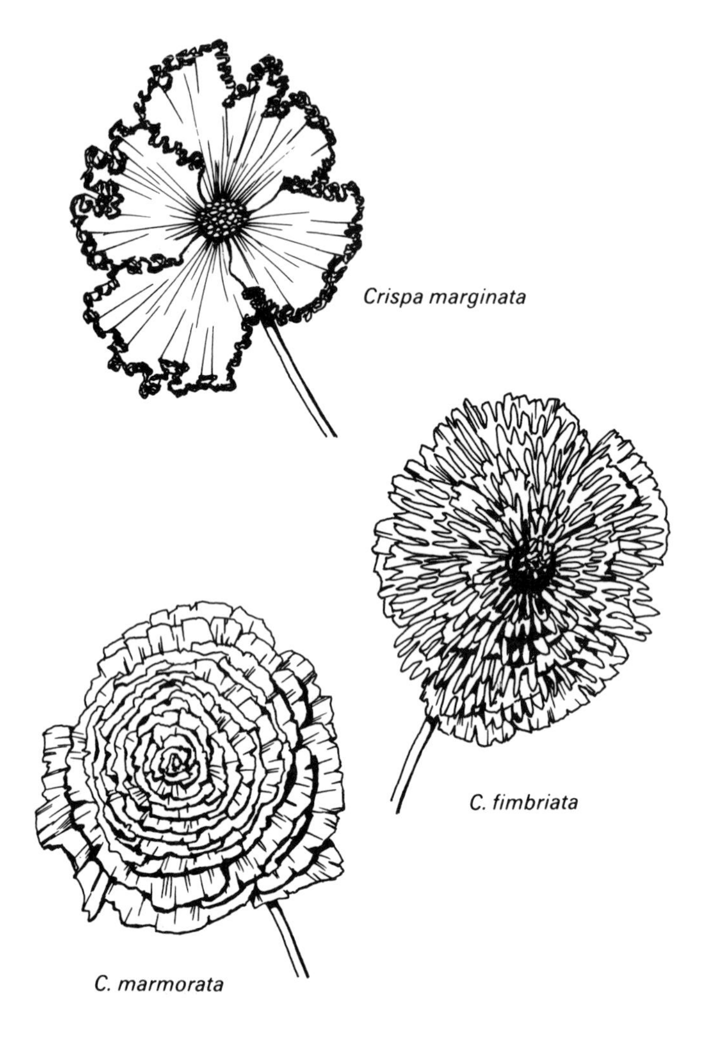

Other Tuberous begonias. The distinctive petal structure or colouring of three types of Tuberhybrida begonias.

white variegated flowers, propagated from seed. Whilst undoubtedly the situation with regard to Marmorata begonias is not very healthy, it is not quite as bad as that. Tubers of double Marmorata begonias can be purchased (varying in shades of carmine), and it is my belief that seed sold under the title 'Double Marbled Mixed' is in reality identical to the Marmorata group. You can expect 75 per cent double flowers in carmine, crimson, pink and orange marbled and speckled with white.

The flowers of the Marmorata group measure some 4in (10cm) in diameter, and stand above the foliage on plants which are similar in form to the large-flowered double types. They scorch fairly easily when in direct midday sunlight, but in a shady spot make most attractive container plants for the patio.

Their cultivation is identical to that described in Chapter 3, both from seed and tubers, except that it is unusual and unnecessary to remove the female buds.

FIMBRIATA BEGONIAS

Two years before the end of the nineteenth century the first double-begonia with frilled petals, was discovered in Belgium. To this begonia and those which followed it the name Fimbriata was given. Over the following 10–15 years a number of improved hybrids were added to the list, with the colour range being extended to include white, pale pink, salmon, red, and orange. At the same time the petal structure was changing from frilled to being finely serrated so that each individual was apparently fringed, and resembled a carnation. Much later the yellow-coloured Fimbriata begonias were added to the list.

The present day Fimbriata begonias have such extensive fimbriation that it is no longer very easy to see the defined petals, whereas the very first plant in this group had merely frilled or ruffled petals.

Around the 1950s the American firm of Vetterle & Reinelt introduced their ruffled, large-flowered, double-begonias which, though far more perfect in form, did have a similar frill to the petals. Similar frilled (ruffled) petal types are available today in varieties such as 'Jenny Barclay', 'Sea Coral', 'Tahiti', etc. In Australia the firm of Ralph Willsmore have the varieties 'Flo' Willsmore' and 'Blushing Bride', both of which are very extensively ruffled. There is little doubt that these named varieties within the large-flowered, double-begonia group have been developed from the early Fimbriata types.

The Fimbriata begonias may be grown from seed or from tubers, though in the former case they may be listed as fringed double mixed. Their cultivation is exactly as for the Marmorata types.

CRISPA MARGINATA BEGONIAS

This group consists of only two members, and the flowers are single, heavily fringed with bright-red margins. The base colour of the flower is either white or yellow. Interestingly enough the very first reported example of the Crispa marginata group had a red base colour with a white edge. This is an unusual colour reversal from the normal picotee arrangement where the deeper colour is that of the margin. Today the only two types available are the white and the yellow ground colour with red margins, though considerable differences can be seen in the various shades of red. These have been catalogued as 'Helvetica' and 'Belgica' respectively, though these names are not in general use. They may be grown from seed or from tubers, and are cultivated exactly as described above. They really should be pot grown or at the worst in containers for patio work since they can suffer greatly from sun and wind damage.

Each of these Tuberous begonia groups can provide examples of most attractive and worthwhile greenhouse flowering plants. Individual plants from these groups should be in every begonia enthusiast's collection, and perhaps also they are worthy of being investigated by keen amateur hybridizers. The firm of Vetterle and Reinelt certainly felt that developing the ruffled type of begonia was a reasonable exercise but, unfortunately, their stock was dissipated when the nursery ceased to trade.

7
CANE-STEMMED BEGONIAS

The begonias so far discussed have in common the fact that they are cultivated almost entirely for their flowers. Whether they are grown outdoors (the Semperflorens), or under glass (the Tuberous doubles and singles, or the Hiemalis types), deciding which ones to grow is based almost exclusively on the colour and quality of bloom. Just occasionally, however, one takes into consideration the foliage colour in the case of the Semperflorens, though this is usually very much a secondary matter. Also, many of the begonias already discussed do have a dormant period, or at least a time when growth all but ceases.

PLANT DESCRIPTION

Now, with the Cane-stemmed type, we are dealing with a group of begonias which represent a very wide range of growth habits. They range from a height of only a few inches to those giants which, even in a northern climate, can attain heights of over 10ft (3m). Additionally, though they have particular flowering periods, these are often only loosely defined and many do continue to grow throughout the year, albeit much more slowly during the winter. To maintain this growth through the winter months a degree of artificial heat is required, but one must not get this out of perspective and attempt to provide tropical conditions.

In general the individual flowers are small compared with those described in previous chapters, but they are grouped in fairly large clusters and, together with the most attractive foliage, give a highly pleasing pot plant.

Up to a few years ago this type of begonia, with the exception of one or two notable examples, was usually difficult to obtain, but fortunately a greater selection is now becoming available. The basic characteristic of the Cane-stemmed (or cane-like) begonia is that the stems resemble those of bamboo, having swollen nodes along their length, the distance between the nodes being fairly regular.

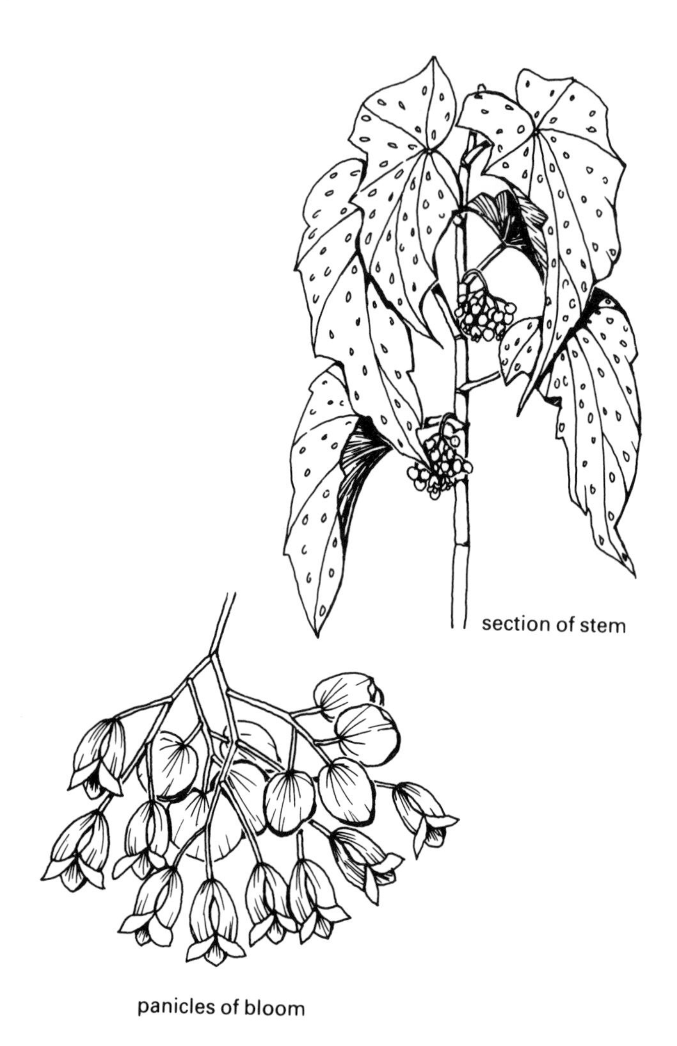

The flowers of this Angel-wing begonia are smallish in size but are carried in drooping panicles.

The stems may be erect or they may be somewhat more pendulous, and they are not very prolific in respect of branching. However, when correctly grown this can be compensated for by the new shoots which come from the base of the plant. In America it has become popular to sub divide the Cane-like begonias into three sub-groups: the Superba type, the Mallet type, and 'others'. A further sub division of the latter group is made according to their mature height, but this is not normally followed in Britain.

At the present time there are something like 250–300 hybrids and species cultivated and, unlike the begonias already discussed, many of the species are still highly valued as house- and pot plants. Though without doubt many of today's hybrids show a marked improvement on the species they do not, in general, reflect such a departure from their parents as do the large-flowered, Tuberous doubles from their origins. It is possible to generalize on the growing conditions needed for this group of begonias, and to indicate how the specific sub-groups differ from the general.

CULTIVATION

In Britain all Cane-stemmed begonias need to be grown in a protective environment such as a greenhouse, conservatory, or in the home. They can survive low temperatures as long as they are above freezing, but growth will cease entirely and it will indeed be very slow at anything less than about 45°F (7.5°C). The most satisfactory temperature range is from 50°F (10°C) to around 75°F (24°C), though they will not suffer too much if at the hottest point of the day temperatures rise considerably above this level. But it is absolutely essential that if high temperatures are to be withstood, the begonias have adequate atmospheric humidity and plenty of water at the roots. A humidity of some 45–65 per cent would be ideal, and these conditions are best achieved in a protected growing environment. When the humidity is about right then the leaves are soft and flexible, but when there is insufficient moisture then they become much more brittle and hard.

Perhaps the most important single factor is, however, the amount of light which is given to the plant. Though direct sunlight will quickly scorch the foliage it is absolutely essential that the plants are given the maximum light possible to encourage flower production. It is not easy to ensure that sufficient light is available to plants which are being grown in the house – certainly the leaves adjacent to the window will be fine, but those pointing into the room will be deprived of adequate light which could severely restrict the amount of flower produced. In a greenhouse or conservatory, however, the plants should receive sufficient light from all angles. Those plants grown in insufficient light will have disappointingly few flowers and stems which are drawn and weak.

Repotting, Growth, Feeding and Pruning

Though it is quite possible to grow the Cane-stemmed begonias in peat-based composts it is generally found that they do prefer a growing medium which contains loam, and therefore John Innes No 2 or 3 is suggested. In any case since these plants do grow rather tall the heavier compost will help to stabilize them. Perhaps more than all the begonias already discussed the Cane-stemmed types resent being overpotted, and for the first two years a 5in (13cm) pot is probably adequate. Purely because of the weight involved a crock pot is preferable. Repotting should be carried out only when the pot is full of root and then only into the next size which will greatly help to increase the amount of flower produced.

During the summer months growth should be quite rapid and with the taller varieties a height of perhaps 4–5ft (1.2–1.5m) could be rapidly attained. Partly to restrict the height, but also to encourage branching, the growing points should be pinched out. However, 'stopping' a plant in this way sometimes results in the main stem breaking into growth again from a node lower down.

With the more vigorous Cane-stemmed begonias no pruning is required for about three years, but then it will be necessary to reduce the overall size of the plant and to encourage more basal growths. Pruning is done by cutting the stems cleanly with secateurs at a point about three to four nodes from the base, and preferably where there is an outward facing bud or 'eye'.

As with all growing plants Cane-stemmed begonias will benefit greatly from regular feeding with a balanced fertilizer, but only during the period of active growth. Though this type of begonia does not have a real dormant season, growth will slow down considerably when the temperature falls and daytime light levels are low. During these periods no feeding should be carried out. High nitrogen feeds will encourage somewhat spindly growth and should be avoided. A 20:20:20 fertilizer, given at half strength once a week, will be adequate to maintain good, balanced growth. Switching to a fertilizer higher in potash one month before the major flowering period can also be helpful in increasing the yield of bloom.

Where watering is concerned this type of begonia does not like to be grown in overwet conditions otherwise it will respond by dropping its lower leaves in protest! Watering is carried out only when it is clear that the compost is on the point of drying out. During the winter watering is reduced even further to the point of merely keeping the plant alive. The main groups of Cane-stemmed begonias will now be considered in more detail:

SUPERBA

These hybrids are characterized by their rather tall, slender stems and heavily lobed, cleft-wavy edged leaves. The leaf colour is usually dark to bronzy green, and often the upper surface is marbled or splashed with silver or silvery pink markings, though in the early stages of growth this may not appear. Pruning is essential if the plants are to be kept to a reasonable height since this group tends to be taller than the other Cane-stemmed types.

The development of this group goes back to approximately 1926 when, in California, Eva Gray crossed the species *B. aconitifolia* with the hybrid B. 'Lucerna' (an Angel-wing, Cane-stemmed begonia) to produce a number of new hybrids – B. 'Superba-Azella', B. 'Superba-Mentone' and B. 'Superba-Kenzii'. Since then many other hybrids have been produced and are still being registered from time to time.

The very early hybrids had a distinct tendency to become dormant in the winter, presumably due to the influence of *B. aconitifolia*, but in the modern hybrids this tendency is almost completely suppressed. The later hybrids are also extremely floriferous with large panicles of white or pink blooms. The Superba hybrids need to be pruned to keep their height to manageable proportions, and regular pinching out of growing points will achieve a well-proportioned plant since bareness on the lower stems is fairly common.

Though the name Superba was introduced to identify a group of hybrids which had foliage so markedly different from the Mallet and the Angel-wing types, it was clear that a number of species could also be identified as having very similar characteristics. These were referred to as 'Superba species'.

The one or two species in this group which are still grown are difficult to keep compact, and have a pronounced tendency to go into dormancy through the winter. Nonetheless, with regular feeding and proper care and attention they can provide a most attractive plant.

Cultivars and Species

B. aconitifolia

A Brazilian species with silky green leaves deeply cut, and with faint silvery markings. The white flowers flushed pink are produced in late autumn.

B. 'Esther Albertine'
Deeply cut, waxy, mid-green leaves and pink flowers produced freely all year round. This is a cross of *B. sceptrum* (itself a Superba species) with B. 'Lenore Olivier' (a low-growing Cane-stemmed begonia).

B. 'Irene Nuss'
Yet another B. 'Lenore Olivier' cross, this time with B. 'Kentwood' (itself a *B. sceptrum* cross), with dark-green/bronze leaves, deeply cut and splashed with silvery-pink. The flowers, borne in quantity from April until December, are coral pink and said to be fragrant.

B. leathermaniae
A new species from Bolivia – the deeply cut leaves are emerald green, splashed with a much deeper green. Where the leaf joins the petiole there is a ring of fine hairs. The pale-pink flowers which are produced rarely occur in large clusters.

B. 'Nokomis'
A B. 'Lana' cross with light-green leaves heavily splashed with silver. The pale-pink flowers are produced from April to October.

B. platanifolia
A tall-growing species (up to 5ft – 1.5m) from Brazil. The large, velvety green leaves are deeply cleft and a purple-tinted light green below. The off-white flowers are produced somewhat sparingly in November/December.

B. 'Sophie Cecile'
Another B. 'Lenore Olivier' cross with *B. sceptrum*. The rose-pink flowers are produced through the summer months and are claimed by some to be fragrant.

B. teuscheri
A species from Surinam, discovered in 1879, which has thick olive-green leaves spotted white and a resemblance to *B. metallica*. Its pink flowers are produced in late summer/autumn.

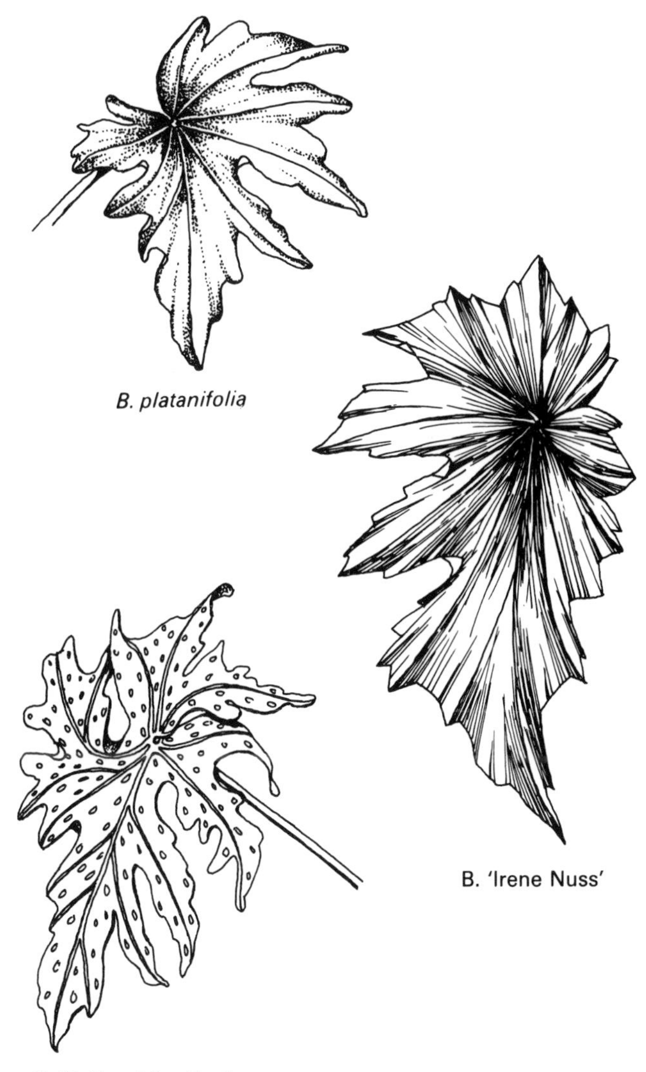

Superba leaf shapes. The leaves of the Superba types of Cane-stemmed begonias are deeply serrated.

MALLET

This is not a very large group, but the members of it are sufficiently different from the other Cane-stemmed begonias to warrant a separate listing. The cultivation for this group is basically as described above, with one or two slight differences – for example they do not like quite as much direct sun, and they prefer a somewhat higher atmospheric humidity. Staking is often necessary since the stems are less substantial than the Superba types. The Mallet types are recognizable by their mahogany-coloured foliage, the leaves often having a slightly serrated or saw edge.

All the plants in this group are hybrids, one of the very first being B. 'Arthur Mallet', a cross of B. rex 'Eldorado' with *B. subpeltata* made in 1884. The latter, according to Chevalier, is a Rhizomatous type which, when crossed with *B. socotrana*, gave rise to B. 'Gloire de Sceaux' (which is a Shrub-like begonia). This strange background suggests that the crossing of a Rex with a Rhizomatous begonia gave rise to a whole new group of Cane-stemmed hybrids, of which B. 'Arthur Mallet' was one of the first.

Of the cultivars still grown today the following are perhaps the best known:

B. 'Gloire de Jouy'

A cross of a Rex cultivar with *B. incarnata*. This hybrid has green/bronze foliage which is covered with silvery spots. The pale-pink flowers are produced in abundance during the winter months.

B. 'Margaritacea'

A cross of B. 'Arthur Mallet' and B. 'Gloire de Sceaux'. The foliage is purple-red overlaid with silver, giving the leaves a metallic appearance. It is a very easy grower being somewhat sturdier than the normal Mallet types, and it appears to be more tolerant of mildew. The flowers are freely produced and are of a bright pink colour.

B. 'Tingley Mallet'

A cross of B. rex 'Eldorado' and *B. incarnata purpurea*, a small bare-leaved, Mexican, Shrub-like species. B. 'Tingley Mallet' is a most attractive begonia with brilliant red/bronze leaves which carry silvery pink spots and which are covered with fine red hairs. The flowers, which are produced from April to October, are rose-pink in colour.

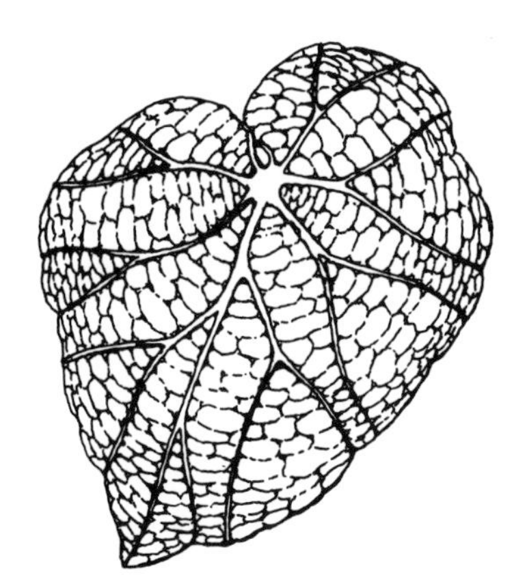

B. 'Tingley Mallet'

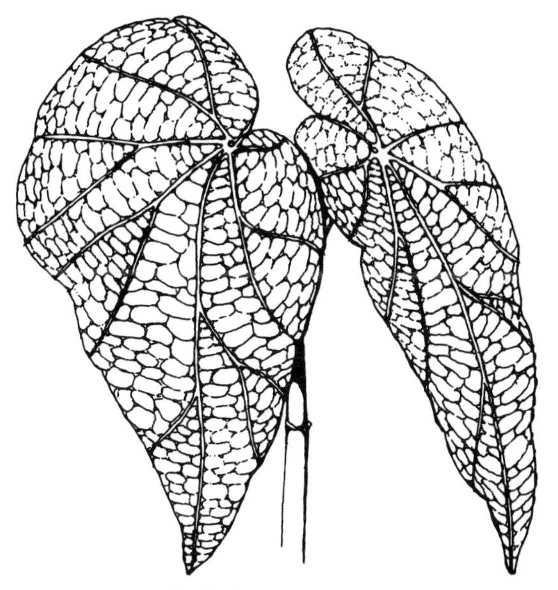

B. 'Arthur Mallet'

Mallet type leaf shapes. Most of the Mallet type of Cane-stemmed begonias have foliage which is mahogany red in colour.

OTHER TYPES

This is the group in which one finds the greatest number of Cane-stemmed begonias, both species and hybrids. In general they are sub divided into tall growing, medium growing, and low growing, but here we shall select just a few of those available and describe their individual habits.

Within this very large group there are quite a number which have been given the trivial but very descriptive name of Angel-wing begonias. This name reflects the fact that pairs of leaves (with one lobe larger and higher than the other) on opposite sides of the main stems closely resemble the traditional representation of angels' wings. Angel-wing begonias are to be found in each of the sub-divisions of this group.

Species

B. albo-picta
Originally from Brazil, and is most probably a variety of *B. maculata*. It grows to about 4ft (1.2m) tall and has small – 3½ × 1in (9 × 2.5cm wide) – shiny green leaves covered with silver spots. The leaf underside is green. The small white flowers are produced in panicles throughout the summer. The plant is bushy but to maintain an attractive example it is better to renew it by propagation every two to three years.

B. angularis
A tall and somewhat elegant species from Brazil. The outstanding feature is the long, narrow leaf slightly waved at the edges, but coloured a most delicate grey/green with a satin-like finish and red underneath. The veins on the upper side are grey. The white flowers are not very impressive.

B. coccinea
Another Brazilian species which, in its native state, can reach up to 15ft (4.5m) tall, but in cultivation has to be restricted according to the space available. The leaves are bright green and unspotted. The flowers can vary from deep coral pink to bright red, and are carried in large clusters. This species has been widely used in the production of many hybrids.

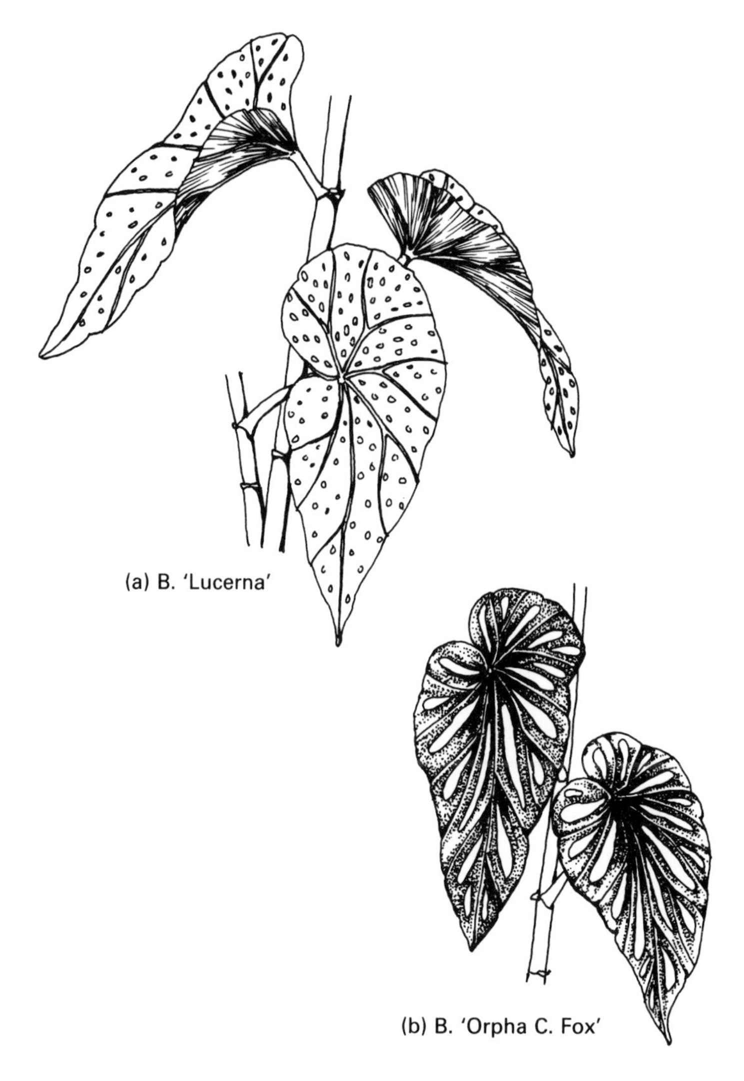

Two typical Cane-stemmed begonias: (a) with silver spotted; and (b) with silver splashed leaves.

B. dichroa

A short growing plant (12–14in – 30–35cm tall) with bright green leaves which may be silver spotted when young. The plant habit is somewhat pendulous and the stems carry brilliant orange flowers throughout the year. Needs to be kept warm through the year and resents being placed in draughty conditions. This is the species which has given the orange colouration to many hybrids.

B. lubbersii

A fairly low-growing (about 20in – 50cm tall) begonia species from Brazil. The leaves are narrow, 6in (15cm) long by 2in (5cm) wide, pointed at both ends and joined to the petiole near the centre. The dark-green leaves are often splashed with silver spots which tend to disappear with age. The large, fragrant flowers are white in colour, but tinted pink or salmon, and are produced intermittently throughout the year.

B. maculata

A Brazilian species which can grow to a height of 10ft (3m) but is usually restricted to about 3ft (90cm) by extensive pinching out of the growing points. The 8in (20cm) long, and 3in (7.5cm) narrow lobed leaves are dark olive green/silver, spotted and red on the reverse. The flowers, borne in panicles, are pale pink. The variety *wightii* is similar in habit but has greenish white flowers.

Hybrids

B. 'Corallina de Lucerna'

This is probably the most widely cultivated Angel-wing begonia, and one of the earliest hybrids dating back to 1892. Can be a very tall grower and needs to be restricted to about 5ft (1.5m) high by pinching out the growing tip. The leaves are large, dark green, and heavily spotted silver. Flowers can be produced at almost any time of the year, but the heaviest yield is in the midsummer period when large clusters of coral-pink blooms are quite spectacular. Known more commonly as 'Lucerna'.

B. 'Di-Anna'

A cross of *B. dichroa* with B. 'Annie Laurie', itself a seedling from *B. coccinea*. This is an intermediate growing Cane-stemmed begonia which does not exceed 4ft (1.2m) in height, and may be kept much smaller by judicious pinching and pruning. The green leaves are heavily silver spotted and the flowers, which are borne

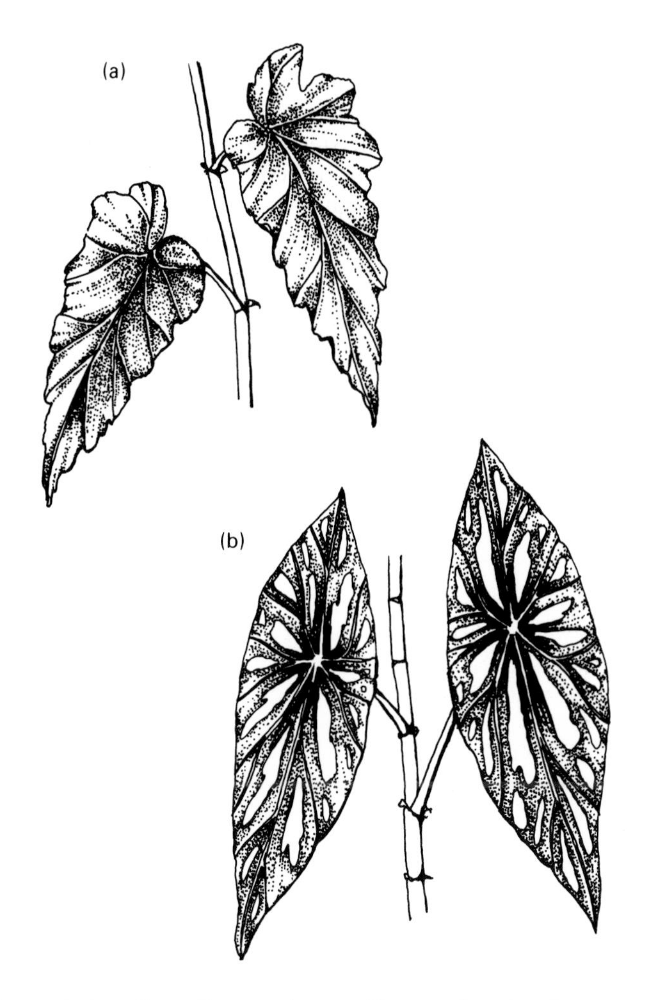

(*a*) B. angularis*, satiny, olive-green leaves with very pale main vein areas – the elongated leaves have wavy margins;* (*b*) B. lubbersii*, the leaves are pointed at both ends and are joined to the leaf stalk almost at their centres.*

throughout the year but at intermittent times, are salmon-orange in colour.

B. 'Di-Erna'

A cross of *B. dichroa* with B. 'Rubra'. It is a tall-growing plant with plain, light-green leaves. It is very free-flowering with deep coral blooms for most of the year.

B. 'Elaine'
A seedling from B. 'Lucerna'. Its leaves are unspotted and very dark red with a tendency for the margins to curl upwards. The flowers, which are produced in very early spring, are rose-pink and carried in large drooping clusters.

B. 'Flo' Belle Moseley'
Like B. 'Pickobeth' it is another cross of *B. dregei* and B. 'Laura Engelbert', but here the habit is more compact and the plant much lower growing. The leaves are dark green, somewhat maple leaf-shaped, and speckled white. From April onwards the plant is covered with large rose-pink flowers.

B. 'Honeysuckle'
This is a Logee *B. dichroa* seedling introduced some 10 years ago. It is an intermediate grower with bright green angel-wing leaves, and rose-pink flowers which are fragrant.

B. 'Orange Parade'
A low-growing hybrid from a cross between *B. dichroa* and *B. rubra*. The foliage is bronze-green and the orange flowers are seen to great effect against this background.

B. 'Orange Rubra'
A famous *B. dichroa* hybrid with B. 'Coral Rubra', produced in 1947, but still eagerly sought after. The light green leaves are unspotted, and the somewhat drooping habit of the slender stems makes the plant very suitable for basket use. The rather showy, brilliant orange flowers are carried in large clusters from spring to late autumn.

B. 'Orpha C. Fox'
This is a seedling from a Superba hybrid B. 'Hanna Serr'. It makes a most attractive and compact plant some 2½ft (76cm) tall, and quite bushy. The leaves are most impressive with their dark, olive-green colour relieved by silver spotting. The rose-pink flowers are freely produced throughout the year, and contrast strongly with the red shades of the stems and the underside of the foliage.

B. 'Orrell'
A much older cross from Luçerna, but still one of the most popular. The long, slender, light green leaves are silver spotted, and the flowers vary from cherry red to salmon-rose.

B. 'Pickobeth'
One of the more recent crosses (1974) of *B. dregei* with B. 'Laura Engelbert'. It is a tall-growing plant with cream/white spots on the deep green leaves. The shocking pink flowers are produced in sprays during the first six months of the year.

B. 'Pink Spot Lucerna'
A cross of 'Lucerna' with *B. dichroa*. It is a much lower growing, Cane-stemmed begonia than its hybrid parent, and the flowers are carmine red in colour. The leaves are spotted metallic pink.

B. 'President Carnot'
Another very early hybrid (1890), but still widely cultivated. This is a tall grower with deep-red flowers produced profusely from April to October.

B. 'Swirly Top'
This is a cross of another Cane-stemmed begonia B. 'Lenore Olivier' with a Rhizomatous species *B. kenworthyae*. It is a low-growing plant with somewhat wavy maroon and green leaves. The pale pink flowers are produced during the winter months but not in great quantity.

B. 'Tom Ment'
This is a cross between B. 'Di-Erna' and B. 'Orange Rubra' obtained approximately 17 years ago, and is still one of the most popular Cane-stemmed varieties. The heavily spotted green leaves make an attractive foil for the profusely borne pink-orange flowers – once the plant begins to flower it seems to go on for ever. This variety is not a tall grower and the rather shapely plant is restricted to a height of some 3½ft (1m).

Some of these low-growing, Cane-stemmed begonias can be used to great effect in hanging baskets. In the early stages of the stem development they are encouraged to trail over the sides of the basket by attaching small weights to the ends of the stems.

In recent years a new race of miniature Cane-stemmed begonias has appeared, introduced by Patrick Worley of California. They grow only a few inches high and are greatly scaled-down versions of their taller cousins. Two which are most attractive and will make very good houseplants are:

B. 'Amber Meyer' ('Mandarin' × *B. suffruticosa* × *B. dregei* 'Lacy')
This has 8–10in (20–25cm) long, pale-green stems carrying light green leaves – 2in (5cm) long by ¾in (20mm) wide – heavily marked with silvery white spots. The coral-pink flowers are borne profusely in summer, though indeed the blooms are found all the year round. The variety produces many basal shoots giving the plant a bushy appearance.

B. 'Kathleen Meyer' ('Mandarin' × *B. homonyma*)
A miniature very similar in habit and foliage to that above but the flowers are reddish pink in colour.

Two others of similar characteristics are B. 'Brandie Meyer' and B. 'Downal Meyer', the former has small green leaves with silver spots, and the latter dark bronze leaves. Both have pink blossoms.

On the whole this is a most attractive group of plants and, in general, fairly easy to grow. They do need an adequate amount of light to get the best from them in terms of flower. In my own experience there is not too much difference in the amount of light required to produce masses of bloom and that which effectively prevents any flowering at all. This is of considerable importance when the plants are grown in the house where just a move of 2ft (60cm) closer to a window can convert a foliage plant into one heavy with flowers.

8
RHIZOMATOUS BEGONIAS

This is a fairly wide group of begonias which includes many different leaf shapes, colours and textures. Though the foliage is undoubtedly the main attraction, nevertheless the flowers – frequently produced in the winter and early spring – are allowed to remain on the plants thus adding to their overall beauty. This is certainly a case where the blooms add an extra dimension to an already most attractive subject.

The number of species and named cultivars already tops the 700 mark, making it the largest single group of begonias. When one adds to this the multitude of unnamed hybrids presently available, then the popularity of this type of begonia becomes clear. This situation is so different from that of the Semperflorens group where the number of cultivars is not unduly high, but where the number of plants grown is extremely large indeed.

The one feature obviously linking all the members of this group is that they grow from a rhizome or thickened stem which grows at, or just below, the compost surface, or in some examples is upright. The leaves and flower stems grow directly from the rhizome which, in the case of the creeping or horizontal types, frequently branches thus increasing the overall size of the plant.

Generally, many of the Rhizomatous begonias whose leaves are incised or cleft, or even parted, and whose colours are principally green or brown with a smooth surface (glabrous), have their origins in Central and South America. Those where the leaf surfaces are textured (pustulate), or where the colours are so distinctive that they clearly set them apart from the others, may originate in Africa, the Americas and Asia, though this division is only of the most general kind and there are many exceptions.

The flowering habit is also quite varied ranging from those whose blooms are held on long flower stems above the plant, to those with flowers buried in the foliage. With a small number of exceptions the Rhizomatous begonias are not very demanding subjects in respect of their growing needs, and make good houseplants. As we shall see two of the most frequently seen houseplants are Rhizomatous hybrids derived from *B. bowerae*, a Mexican species, and almost invariably (but often incorrectly) named 'Cleopatra' and 'Tiger'. Such plants do withstand the most outrageous ill-treatment without succumbing. Under the most adverse conditions they still grow, albeit very poorly, which suggests that they would amply reward more care and attention.

CULTIVATION

Here we shall describe the general cultivation for this group, and note any modifications which are desirable for specific examples. The compost for the Rhizomatous types can be either loam-based or the peat-based variety, as long as it is very free-draining – like most begonias these types do not like having wet roots. In terms of air-filled porosity the 12–15 per cent level is about right.

Potting on should occur fairly frequently, about every six months or so, and for an everage greenhouse plant it should not be necessary to exceed a diameter pot size of 5½in (14cm). At this size a half-pot is better. Of course if you wish to grow a specimen plant the much larger size half-pots can be used. To assist in keeping the compost fairly dry it is better to use a terracotta-type pot rather than a plastic one.

The amount of light needed to cultivate Rhizomatous begonias is an area of some disagreement amongst growers, some stating that the light should be subdued whilst others maintain that as much as possible should be given, but not direct sunlight. Too little light results in leggy growth, whilst excess light produces rather hard and yellow foliage, and poor plant development. As a guideline only, in my own greenhouse (which is sited in open ground) the only shading on that section is 50 per cent shade cloth. Even at the height of the summer, with full sun, the Rhizomatous plants have grown well and kept their healthy green colours. It is the high temperatures, which often accompany such bright conditions, which reduce growth considerably. In a greenhouse it is often necessary to move around the Rhizomatous plants until the best conditions for growth are found. In a British winter these plants can be given almost full sunlight.

Watering is the other area of cultivation which sometimes gives trouble, especially if the grower is heavy handed with the watering-can. Since the very fleshy rhizomes already contain a lot of water the plants can survive for lengthy periods without added liquid. Watering should only be carried out when the compost has actually dried out – overwatering will undoubtedly cause the rhizome to rot, and when this begins it is difficult to save the plant. However, when water is given the plant should be watered thoroughly and then allowed to drain. Watering by immersion is a much lengthier process than top-watering, but it does reduce the probability of rhizome rotting. During the winter, when some Rhizomatous begonias might go into a type of dormant state, a reduction in the amount of water given is essential.

Most Rhizomatous begonias require temperatures of 55–70°F (13–21°C) for optimum growth, though they will tolerate levels higher or lower than this for short periods.

As far as atmospheric humidity is concerned Rhizomatous begonias are not too demanding, and they will thrive in a humidity of 50–60 per cent. However, at the height of the summer the humidity can fall to well below this range and requires the addition of water through misting nozzles.

During the main growing season the plants should be fed regularly (once each week) with a fertilizer of NPK 15:15:30, and at half strength. No feeding is required during the winter months.

Purely for reasons of convenience we shall separate the Rhizomatous begonias into two groups – those which have glabrous or near-glabrous leaves (which may be glossy or satiny), and those which have interesting leaf surfaces or decorative leaf colouring.

GLABROUS OR NEAR GLABROUS

Most examples of this type have rhizomes which grow horizontally (creeping), and which have a pronounced tendency to branch as they go, thus forming a dense plant quite quickly. Since the foliage rises upwards from the rhizome the plant rapidly assumes a domed structure and it becomes difficult to water from above – watering by immersion is therefore far safer. Also, the leaves can be small, under 2in (5cm) long; intermediate, up to 6in (15cm) long; or large, above 6in (15cm) in length; and they may be plain or spiral, or even crested.

The small-leaved cultivars make good houseplants because they never become large plants, and indeed when they reach the 6in (15cm) pot stage it is probably time to divide them.

Within this sub-group a number of species are grown, but by far the greatest proportion are hybrids derived from the Mexican *B. bowerae*, a small-leaved creeping rhizome type with bright-green leaves splashed on the margins with dark brown. Along the leaf margins are tiny hairs which have given this species, along with many of its offspring, the trivial descriptive name of 'eyelash'. The following is a small selection of the most readily available members of this group, which numbers many hundreds:

B. 'Baby Perfection'
A cross of 'Cleopatra' with *B. bowerae*. It is a true miniature hybrid having tiny leaves measuring ½in (13mm) across.

B. 'Beatrice Hadrell'
This is a cross of *B. bowerae* with *B. sunderbruchii*. It has small star-shaped leaves, almost black in colour, with a bright, light-green sinus that radiates green shading along the leaf veins. The large pink flowers are produced in spring on long, slender stems towering above the foliage.

B. 'Black Watch'
The leaves are deeply cut giving a star-like appearance, almost black in colour and with depressed green veins, red on the reverse, and measuring 4 × 3in (10 × 7.5cm). The whole plant is quite compact growing to a height of 9in (23cm). The large pink flowers are carried on stems some 10in (25cm) tall.

B. bowerae
A species growing to 12in (30cm). The bright-green leaves are edged with plain chocolate brown 'stitching', and there are fine white hairs along the margins. The variety *nigramarga* has leaves of a slightly different shade of green. Both the species and its variety produce, from January onwards, masses of delicate white/pink flowers held well above the foliage.

B. 'Cleopatra'
This is a most popular and readily available *bowerae* hybrid. The medium size, satiny, mid-green leaves are deeply cut giving a star-like appearance. The leaves are splashed with gold and chocolate coloured markings. This is a very amenable cultivar readily producing a mounded plant needing the minimum of attention.

B. 'Erythrophylla'
Known as the 'Beafsteak' and occasionally called 'Feastii'. The almost round leaves are deep green, polished to a high-gloss finish, with mahogany red on the underside with a texture reminiscent of leather. The sport 'Helix' is a spiral version of this hybrid, known

popularly as 'Corkscrew'. 'Bunchii' is a frilled version of the same plant. All are extremely easy to grow and appear to resist all attempts to kill them by neglect!

B. manicata

A Mexican species which has an upright rhizome, but which has a pronounced tendency to change its direction of growth frequently thus giving the plant an unsymmetrical appearance. The leaves are almost round, glossy, and light green. On the leaf stem, just below the blade, is a collar of stiff red hairs or bristles, and it is this 'cuff' which gives the species its name. A number of varieties of this species are known and widely grown, including var. *crispa* which has all-green leaves but with a crested edge, and *aureo-maculata* which has green leaves blotched with yellow or cream. All the varieties carry the collar of hairs on the leaf stem.

B. 'Norah Bedson'

A cross probably of *bowerae* with *daedalea*, created in 1959 by F.J. Bedson, one of the founder members of the National Begonia Society. It is an easily grown variety rapidly making a large plant – the leaves at maturity measure 3 × 2in (7.5 × 5cm), and are bright green with chocolate brown markings. The small pink flowers are carried well above the foliage in early spring.

B. prismatocarpa

A South American species with small, notched, light-green leaves surmounted with yellow flowers throughout the year. Unfortunately this species does need to be grown in the protected environment of a terrarium.

B. 'Red Spider'

An M.L. McIntyre cultivar. The 4½ × 3in (11 × 7.5cm) leaves are heart-shaped with green and with red veins, slightly wavy margins, and a prominent red spot at each sinus. The flowers, produced from January to April, are pink on 12in (30cm) long stems.

B. 'Red Tracery'

Another McIntyre cross. The 2¾ × 4in (7 × 10cm) leaves (occasionally star-shaped) are brown/green and covered in a red spider web pattern, with the red spot at the sinus. The leaf petioles are some 8in (20cm) long. The flowers, produced in January are quite large being up to 1in (2.5cm) across, white or pale pink in colour, and are held well above the foliage.

B. 'Tiger'
Probably more correctly named 'Tiger Paws', though it is the name given to a large number of Rhizomatous begonias of similar characteristics and sold through garden centres. The leaves are approximately 3 × 2in (7.5 × 5cm) and are basically chocolate brown, splashed on each segment with light green. The leaf margins are 'eyelashed'.

UNUSUAL LEAF SURFACES OR COLOURING

As already noted many of these species originate in both South America and Asia, and they form a most interesting group of plants. Some are better grown as terrarium subjects, which means that the closed environment enables the correct atmospheric humidity (around 70 per cent) and temperature to be maintained. In general they should always be watered from beneath (by immersion) since they do not enjoy wet foliage. With one or two exceptions this group prefers to be grown in a somewhat higher temperature range, say 70–75°F (21–24°C) than their smooth-leaved relations.

B. acetosa
A Brazilian species which has rounded leaves, up to 6in (15cm) across, on short substantial stems. The upper sides of the leaves are velvety and green, and ruby red below. This species requires quite a high humidity if the leaf edges are not to curl. Sprays of white flowers are produced in the spring. The plant will rest during the winter when the compost needs to be kept just moist. Not the easiest plant to keep growing, but certainly worth while.

B. cathayana
A species from China. The leaf stems are green and covered in white hairs, the 7 × 4in (2.1 × 10cm) leaves are rounded, gently terminating in a point, and are slightly saw-edged. The beauty of the species is in the colouring of the leaves which are soft, velvety, and dark olive green with areas of lighter green and red veins. Underneath the leaves are wine red, the whole effect being enhanced when sunlight filters through them. The flowers produced in later autumn or early winter are salmon-orange. Like the previous

Multiflora begonia, 'Helen Harms'.

Semperflorens begonia, 'Olympia Salmon Orange'.

Multiflora begonia – orange semi-double.

Pendula begonia, 'Pink Cascade'.

Hiemalis begonia, 'White Melody'.

Hiemalis begonia 'Baluga'.

Hiemalis begonias in a commercial nursery.

Cane-stemmed begonia – miniature angel wing, 'Amber'.

Cheimantha begonia, 'Gloire de Lorraine'.

Tuberous begonia, Crispa marginata.

Rex begonia, *'Silver Queen'*.

B. × tuberhybrida, *'Krakatoa'*.

B. × tuberhybrida, *'Golden Bali Hi'*.

B. × tuberhybrida, *'Dorothy White'*.

B. × tuberhybrida, *'Jennifer Wilson'*.

Twelve cut blooms.

A begonia stand at the Portsmouth and Southsea Show.

species, *cathayana* needs that little extra warmth and humidity. It also needs a rest period when the watering must be cut down drastically, and a few leaves may fall. Again, like the previous two species, the amount of light given in the summer months should be carefully watched since too much will affect the colouring of the leaves.

B. imperialis
A species from Mexico with rounded leaves which taper gently to a point, and are about 4in (10cm) long. The short, green, creeping rhizome is covered with tiny hairs. The colour of the leaves is chocolate brown, with an emerald green shading along the main and subsidiary veins. The texture of the foliage is plush velvet. The flowers, produced sparsely, are white and insignificant, and occur during the autumn and winter. The var. *smaragdina* differs since the leaves are smoother but entirely emerald green.

B. masoniana
A Malayan species with large, puckered, mid-green leaves and a pronounced central brown/black marking, roughly in the shape of a cross (hence the common name 'Iron Cross'). It grows easily and rapidly as a houseplant, but is susceptible to mildew.

B. paulensis
A species from Brazil with shield-shaped mid-green leaves. The veins radiating from the sinus are criss-crossed with secondary veins giving the effect of a spider's web, and the leaf surface within the web is blistered.

B. pustulata
A Mexican species with plain green blistered leaves. The var. *pustulata argentea*, in which the green leaves are splashed with silver streaks, is the one more commonly seen. It needs plenty of warmth and humidity.

B. rajah
A small species from Malay which needs to be grown in an enclosed environment, needing the extra warmth and humidity provided. The small 2 × 2in (5 × 5cm) leaves are bullate (blistered) bronzy green, with a network of yellowish green veins; the underside is a mahogany brown. The flowering season is summer, and the small pink flowers are borne just above the foliage.

The Rhizomatous group of begonias is a most interesting one and can be invaluable for home cultivation (especially the *B. bowerae* hybrids). The shapes, colours, patterns and textures of the foliage is such that almost everyone's taste can be satisfied.

9
REX BEGONIAS

The accidental discovery of Begonia *rex* growing in an orchid pot imported into England 150 years ago rapidly led to this now large, and quite spectacular, group of begonias.

The parent Begonia *rex* is a native of India and Assam and has virtually no leaf stems, the petioles arising in clusters from an underground creeping rhizome. The 9 × 5in (23 × 13cm) leaves are deep green with a metallic lustre, and tinged with purple at or near the leaf margins. The flowers, which are not prolifically produced, are quite large and pale rose in colour. The species grows at quite high elevations of 700–3,000ft (215–900m) in areas which are known for their high rainfall.

About the time that B. *rex* was being introduced to Europe from Assam, a number of other recently discovered Asiatic Rhizomatous begonias were also being imported. Amongst these were:

B. griffithii
A Rhizomatous species from Bhutan with large dark-green leaves, with a wide band of silver grey and dark purple margins.

B. robusta
Originally from Java. The large leaves, together with the leaf stems, are covered with fine red hairs.

B. rubro-venia
Has dark, satiny, green leaves of medium size, spotted white. Also an Indian species.

B. xanthina
Comes from India and has large leaves, dark green above and purple on the reverse. A variety of this species is var. *pictifolia* from Assam, where the leaves are distinguished by the silver markings between the veins; a second variety is var. *lazuli*, where the upper surface of the leaves is a metallic maroon/green, tinged with blue.

Crossing these and other Asiatic species gave rise to an increasing number of exciting new Rhizomatous cultivars. Soon further species from America and China were introduced into the hybrids, thus extending the colour range, the leaf texture, the plant habit, the hardiness of the cultivars, etc. Though it is clear that the majority of today's hybrids are of extremely complex ancestry, indicating that many other types of begonia have been used to good effect, nonetheless they are still Rhizomatous in character. However, because their appearance is distinctly different from the other Rhizomatous types they are grouped under the name Rex cultorum or Begonia Rex, or more colloquially Rexes.

Of the very early hybrids produced three or four are still cultivated today: 'B. 'Fireflush' (1866), B. 'Silver Queen' (1875), and B. 'Abel Carriere' (1876), the latter being a *B. evansiana* (tuberous) cross. Whilst many spectacular hybrids have been named and registered with the American Begonia Society by far the greatest number being sold today in garden centres and supermarkets are unnamed seedlings, purchased on the basis of their looks. Visiting a number of nurseries and garden centres soon reveals a whole clutch of almost identically coloured Rexes, and indeed many growers can hardly differentiate between them, or for that matter between them and known, named varieties.

A typical example of this confusion is the cultivar 'Merry Christmas'. Its leaves are satiny red with a broad, bright-green margin, and a maroon centre and leaf edge. This colour combination is most attractive and can be seen on many dozens of unnamed Rexes purchased in a local garden centre, but all of them slightly differ in some small degree from the named variety. Because of similarity it is not unusual for the purchaser to name his/her plant say 'Merry Xmas', 'Santa' or 'Happy New Year', so that very quickly the horticultural world becomes confused with many almost identical plants bearing associated but different names. It is therefore not surprising that so many seedlings are purchased on the basis of their colour and texture, though it has to be said that the appearance of the adult plants is often quite different from that of the young seedlings.

The common names which have been given to the Rex begonias such as 'painted' and 'Pallet', reflect the reason for their enormous popularity. Extensive hybridization has produced plants with a bewildering range of colours and textures. Here we find blues, reds, greens, greys, purples, etc., overlaid with golden, silver and bronze sheens, and in many different textures (silky, satin, velvet, pustular, and hairy). There is almost no end to the combination of colour, texture and finish possible in this group of begonias.

The size of the Rex begonias can vary from the giant leaf types at

10–12in (25–30cm), through the medium leaf at 6in (15cm), down to the miniatures which are smaller than 3in (7.5cm). The development of the miniature Rexes illustrates a little of the complexity of their ancestry (as mentioned above). This new race of plants has been brought about by crossing some of the large- and medium-leaved Rexes with Tuberous and Semi-tuberous begonias. For example, both 'Baby Rainbow' and 'Ethel Arnold' are crosses of *B. dregei*, and 'Red Zephyr' and 'Firedance' are a result of crossing with *B. suffruticosa*, both of these species being Semi-tuberous African types. A third, African Semi-tuberous species *B. socotrana* has also been used for the same purpose.

Though the vast majority grow from creeping rhizomes there are a number which have either an erect rhizome or even a branching stem. It is usual to sub divide the Rex begonias into the large- and medium-leaved types, the miniatures, and spiral or non-spiral leaved. Spiral-leaved types are those which have one leaf lobe which curls round and overlaps the other, more or less like a corkscrew.

The Rex begonias are not the easiest to grow, needing just the right amount of warmth, light and moisture to bring them to their ultimate potential, though the effect is well worth while. They must be cultivated either in the home (where they make excellent houseplants) or in a heated greenhouse or conservatory; in Britain they cannot be grown outdoors.

CULTIVATION

Though the initial species B. *rex* originated in a region known for its high annual rainfall, this does not mean that today's hybrids like to be grown in wet conditions. In fact the reverse is true. The Rexes like to be grown in a very well-drained compost, but one where moisture is always present. A peat-based medium is ideal, especially if the air-filled porosity is increased to some 20 per cent by the incorporation of additional grit.

Grit has an advantage over perlite since it helps to add to the weight of the pot and thus assists in stabilizing it, preventing the plant from falling over. To help reduce the wetness of the compost it is also advantageous to use crock half-pots, or pans, rather than plastic ones. The growing medium should not be allowed to dry out and watering should be carried out just before the soil becomes parched. Since most Rexes are Rhizomatous, and prone to rotting, it is beneficial to water by immersion when required.

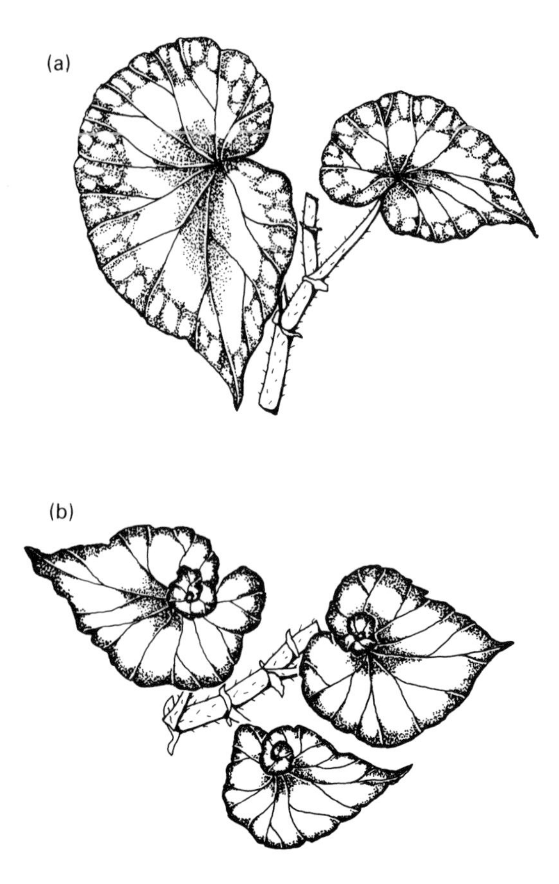

Begonia rex *types: (a) is a non-spiral leaved* B.rex; *(b) is a spiral leaved* B.rex *where the basal leaf lobes overlap.*

When choosing a Rex begonia it is better to select a vigorous variety whenever possible, and preferably one with crisp and strong leaves rather than one with limp, thin foliage. It is a definite disadvantage to purchase a Rex in the autumn since, as we shall see, there is a distinct possibility that it might go dormant at the onset of winter and before there has been ample opportunity to establish the plant in your growing conditions. Early spring is the best time to purchase a Rex if it is at all possible.

The Rex prefers to be grown in warm conditions at about 70°F (21°C), and with sufficient atmospheric humidity to keep the foliage supple. Any crisp browning of the leaf margins indicates an atmosphere which is too dry. When it comes to estimating the correct amount of light, the state of the foliage will indicate what is needed. In general terms the Rex begonias do prefer shady conditions, and many growers find that growing them under the benches is highly satisfactory, whilst others feel that the low light levels in this situation lead to very poor colouration in the leaves. Too high a light level certainly causes severe yellowing of the foliage, and must be avoided. In my own greenhouse I have found that the Rexes do best on the bench when surrounded by taller and bushier plants. Some of the miniature Rexes, and those with more delicate foliage, are particularly suitable for growing under fluorescent lighting when the colours seem to be especially enhanced.

To maintain the rich colouring of a Rex it is advisable to feed regularly during the period of growth. Any balanced fertilizer, applied at half strength every two weeks, will benefit the plant, as will two applications of a chelated iron compound during the season of growth.

As noted Rex begonias normally grow as a creeping rhizome which branch as they progress, soon filling the surface of the compost. Repotting, however, should be delayed until the pot is virtually root bound. A rhizome sitting in an oversize pot does appear to be susceptible to rotting. Also note that from time to time flowers will appear and, unless they are needed for hybridization, should be removed as soon as possible.

Since the Rex prefers a warm, humid, growing environment one of the associated problems is the appearance of mildew. At the very worst this will ultimately kill the plant, but even in small amounts it will spoil the appearance by the unsightly marks on the leaves. Though it is always desirable to keep water off the foliage, you should spray with a suitable fungicide (Nimrod-T or one containing Dinocap) at intervals of three weeks from March onwards.

Quite a number of Rex begonias demonstrate a marked tendency to go into dormancy at the onset of autumn, and to re-emerge in spring. This may or may not be related to the fact that many Rex hybrids contain a certain amount of Tuberous ancestry in their breeding. If the temperatures are allowed to fall in the winter then almost all Rexes will become dormant and shed their leaves. However, if the rhizome remains plump and firm the plant will return into growth the next spring. All that is required is that the rhizome must be kept very slightly moist and reasonably warm.

As we have noted, many begonia Rex hybrids have naturally branching rhizomes though there are a number (especially older varieties) where this tendency is not well developed. With these latter types it is necessary to pinch out the growing tips of the rhizomes to encourage branching, and the production of a more compact plant. With increased branching the plant foliage will become quite dense which emphasizes the need to water by immersion, and not by top application. Constant grooming of the plants will be required involving removing debris from the centre of the plant and compost surface to reduce the possibility of botrytis. The removal of leafless rhizomes will also help keep the plants looking fresh.

Rex begonias are amongst the most attractive and startling houseplants, and they appear to thrive in centrally heated houses especially if they are kept in the more humid environment of a bathroom, or standing on a tray of wet gravel.

Listed below are some of the choice, named, Rex begonias, categorized in terms of leaf size and whether they are plain or spiral leaved. The colour descriptions must be taken as approximately correct, remembering that the precise leaf colours will vary somewhat according to the exact light conditions provided.

Miniatures

'Baby Rainbow'
A delightful miniature with leaves in a rainbow of colours.

'Granny'
An upright plant with leaves in silver, pink and red.

'Mini Merry'
Almost identical markings to those of 'Merry Christmas', but with miniature leaves.

'Red Berry'
Foliage bright red all over, and an excellent variety.

'Red Zephyr'
Maple-like leaves, dark green with maroon-coloured centre and leaf margins. Sometimes there is a tendency to spiral leaves.

These miniatures are more difficult to grow than their larger-leaved relatives, but they do make excellent subjects for terrarium cultivation.

Medium-Leaved Varieties

'Curly Merry Christmas'
Spiral type. There is a satiny red leaf with dark burgundy centre, and a silver band merging into the green margin.

'Fantasy'
Spiral type. The foliage comes in all shades of green, with a silvery centre and bands of emerald green, splashed with silver dots and an olive-green margin.

'Her Majesty'
Almost black leaves with rose-coloured band, the whole leaf having a metallic overlay.

'Mohawk'
Deep-maroon centre and margin on olive-green leaf.

'Mulberry'
A very impressive colour combination – a silver band, flushed with a dark red on an essentially brown leaf.

'Painted Lady'
The eye-catching leaf is covered in splashes of colour, especially reds and greens.

'Purple Petticoats'
Spiral type. A silver leaf with a broad pink band at the margin.

'Stardust'
Medium leaves almost completely deep olive-green, and dusted with silver markings.

'Tweed'
Leaf edges somewhat ruffled, dark-green centre to the leaf, speckled silver, with a broad silver band. Covered in white/silver hairs.

'Winter Sunset'
Very dark centre with a silvery green band flushed pink, merging into emerald green.

Large-Leaved Varieties

'Emerald Giant'
Rich bands of green and brown. An outstandingly impressive variety.

'Fairy'
A pointed leaf essentially brown/black, with lime-green veining tinged pink.

'Green Gold'
Silver green leaf heavily ruffled.

'Helen Lewis'
Deep-wine colour with bands of silver.

'Helen Teupel'
Long pointed leaves in garnet red, brushed with silver.

'Maxine Wilson'
Double spiral leaves in a grey/green colour and pink streaks radiating from the centre.

'Merry Christmas'
Satiny red leaves with bright green edge and deeper maroon centre.

'My Valentine'
Spiralled leaf in creamy green, with a rose-red, heart-shaped centre.

'Princess of Hanover'
A spiral type, with leaves banded in dark and light greens.

'Queen of Hanover'
An old variety almost 100 years old with bands of darker and lighter green. The leaf surface is covered with blush-white fine hairs.

Upright Types

There are a number of upright growing Rex begonias both in the spiral and non-spiral leaved types. Just one or two are listed here.

'Abel Carriere'
Small leaves of silver and green, with a glint of silver in sunlight.

'Annie Robinson'
Almost black leaves relieved in the centre by a metallic-looking area. Leaves are red underneath.

'Fireflush' syn. 'Bettina Rothschild'
A most attractive and much sought after Rex. The leaves are dark green and covered with red hairs, as are the stems, the whole effect being ethereal.

'Silver Fleece'
Light-green leaves marked with silver splashes.

It is perhaps worth restating that, whilst the named varieties described above are undoubtedly very desirable plants to have in one's collection, they are not always easy to find in Britain. On the other hand almost every garden centre and nursery will have many, most attractive unnamed seedlings on sale at very competitive prices, which are just as desirable as the named sorts. From an exhibition point of view they are just as impressive as many of the named kind.

There is no doubt that the Rex cultorum group contains some of the most spectacular subjects to be seen in the world of horticulture, with their fascinating foliage colours and textures. Speaking of the very early Rex hybrids, Chevalier (quoting from the *Journal of Practical Horticulture*, 1858) reports '. . . who has never seen these begonias has never seen a marvel'.

10
MISCELLANEOUS BEGONIAS

There are quite a number of begonias cultivated today which do not fit into the groups already described. In Britain these begonias tend to be dealt with under the all embracing term of 'fibrous-rooted' though, as we have already seen in the introduction, this is quite incorrect. In America it would be more usual to categorize these begonias as Shrub-like, Semi-tuberous and Thick-stemmed (as indeed they are) though here, since we shall be looking at only a small number, they are conveniently described as 'miscellaneous begonias'.

Most of them are quite definitely greenhouse plants, one or two can be cultivated out of doors in a good summer in the south of England, and a few which come from hot, humid parts of the world are best treated as terrarium subjects. Many of the species and hybrids described here are obtainable in England and/or France, though a much greater selection is obtainable from America (as is true of the Rexes).

Of the three groups mentioned above perhaps the Thick-stemmed is the least popular, very few being cultivated except by hybridists. Semi-tuberous begonias are not the most frequently seen plants, but then not many of them are known at the present time. On the other hand the Shrub-like begonias are very widely cultivated, both as species and hybrids.

In this account we shall deal with merely a selection of all three types to illustrate the principles of their cultivation. For information regarding the cultivation of the multitude of species and hybrids not described, the reader will need to consult other texts which cover in greater detail this type of begonia (*see* Bibliography, Appendix IV).

SEMI-TUBEROUS

The main characteristic of this type of begonia is the pronounced swelling of the main stem just at, and below, the compost surface.

In general they do not have a definite period of dormancy and, if the light and temperature levels are adequate, they will continue to grow all the year round. At lower light levels all the leaves may be shed, though this does not necessarily mean that the plant has become dormant (as is the case with the Tuberous types). A dormant period is not a necessary part of the cultivation of these begonias. At temperatures of about 40°F (4.5°C) the leaves will be shed, but the stems will remain on the plant. In the spring when temperatures rise then it is desirable to cut away these leafless stems to encourage new growths to appear.

To ensure a good display of flower provide as much light as can be given short of scorching the foliage. An air temperature of 65°F (18.5°C) is ideal, together with about 45 per cent humidity. The compost should be peat-based, similar to the standard potting mix as described in Chapter 15. As with the Tuberous begonias these plants will produce their best flowering only when the pots are full of root and, at this stage, a potassium-rich fertilizer (NPK 15:15:30) is supplied throughout the growing period every three or four days at quarter strength. Outside the growing period no fertilizer need be given. Perhaps the most difficult part of the cultivation is the question of watering since these plants do not thrive in continuously wet conditions. In fact water should be given only when the compost is becoming dry. In the semi-dormant period even this amount of water should be reduced.

During the growing period the major task is keeping the plants attractive by trimming and pruning. Also, propagation of these plants is preferably achieved by stem cuttings taken in the summer or, in the case of the species, from seed. Just a few typical examples of species and cultivars are given here.

B. dregei

This is a species from South Africa which has been extensively used in the production of winter-flowering begonias. Grown from seed the young, light-green leaves are heavily speckled with white, though the more mature foliage is unmarked. The attractive leaves are maple-shaped, hence the common name 'Maple Leaf'. The flowers borne profusely in the late summer are small and white. One or two select varieties, such as 'Macbethii' and 'Macbethii Obtusa' are also available. *B. dregei* has been used quite considerably in the development of B. Tuberhybrida in an attempt to eliminate the tendency for pink and red shades to appear in the dorsal petals of certain white and yellow cultivars.

(*a*) B. dregei, *a Semi-tuberous begonia with maple-like leaves;* (*b*) B. ludwigii, *a Thick-stemmed type of begonia.*

B. partita

This is another South African (Natal) species and was introduced in 1961. The adult plant is about 12in (30cm) tall, and is covered with olive-green leaves which highlight the dark-red veins. The small, highly branched and bushy plant is most attractive from spring to autumn when it is carrying a mass of white, flushed pink blooms. The species has been given the common name 'Bonsai'. Seeds can be purchased from the usual seedsmen, and are easy to cultivate. Reducing the amount of water and lowering the temperature to 45°F (7.5°C) in the autumn will induce a dormant state.

B. 'Richard Robinson'

Another *B. dregei* seedling, similar in habit to the above. Some reports suggest that the white flowers are produced between December and April, but the plant in my own greenhouse is usually in flower from spring through to the onset of autumn.

B. 'Weltonensis'

A hybrid from crossing *B. sutherlandii* with *B. dregei*. It is an erect grower covered with mid-green leaves which are lobed and notched. The flowers produced from April to November are light pink in colour. If the temperature is allowed to fall below 50°F (10°C) then all the leaves are shed, and at this stage the plant must be kept dry until the following April when the new growth appears. The new growth can be encouraged by pruning the old stems close to the main stem or trunk.

B. wollnyi

Sometimes is referred to as *B. williamsii*, and is a South American (Bolivian) species introduced in 1909. It is readily cultivated from seed. Propagated from seed it produces a very bushy plant with mid-green leaves heavily splashed with white markings. The leaves are of the maple type and are red-veined on the underside. This species drops all its leaves in November, the bare stems remaining until around March when the flowers, pale pink in colour, are produced profusely. The new leaves appear after the flowers have fallen, and any repotting which is necessary must be carried out between the flower and leaf stages. The mature plant achieves a height of 12in (30cm) and increases in size by throwing new shoots from the base of the thick trunk. These new shoots can be used for propagation.

THICK-STEMMED BEGONIAS

In Britain this type of begonia is even more rare than the Semi-tuberous examples. They require growing conditions very similar to the Semi-tuberous plants – as much light as possible without scorching, and a temperature preferably about 60°F (16°C). In general these plants tend to grow into large specimens up to 6ft (1.8m) in height and become difficult to control. In an effort to regulate the growth it is better that the plants become pot-bound and are fed regularly during the growing season with half-strength fertilizer, twice a week. Since the plants can become top-heavy it is preferable to use clay pots and a loam-based compost as the growing medium. To avoid too tall a growth it is helpful to pinch out the growing tips, so encouraging branching and a corresponding reduction in the overall height of the plant. When new growths are developing quickly the old stems can be pruned out.

Thick-stemmed begonias pass into a state of semi-dormancy if the temperature is allowed to fall to 50°F (10°C) or below. At this stage all watering is stopped until signs of the new growth appear in the spring. Just one or two examples will be mentioned here:

B. ludwigii
A species introduced from Ecuador approximately 60 years ago. This Thick-stemmed plant is an example of the type which produces its foliage at the top of the main trunk, closely resembling a palm tree. The medium-size leaves are very deeply incised, mid-green in colour with a rough surface, and heavily veined. The clusters of white flowers are produced on fairly long stalks throughout the summer.

B. olbia
A Brazilian species introduced 100 years ago. It is an example of the hairy-leaved, Thick-stemmed begonia. These plants can manage with less direct sunlight than their bare-leaved relations, though they still need high light to flower well. Ultimately attaining a height of 3ft (90cm) this species is ideal for greenhouse cultivation, though the creamy white flowers are carried on very short stems and tend to be hidden by the foliage. The leaves are tapered with a saw edge and are bronze-green with a satiny surface. As with some other varieties the young leaves are frequently silver spotted, though these marks disappear with age. A somewhat higher winter temperature of 55°F (13°C) is best if this species is to survive a British winter.

B. vitifolia
A Brazilian species introduced into England 170 years ago. This plant can grow to 5ft (1.5m) in height under the right conditions, but can be kept to about 2–3ft (60–90cm) by careful cultivation. The large 8 × 6in (20 × 15cm) leaves are almost horizontal and thick in texture, being velvety green above and covered in numerous greyish hairs. Clusters of small white flowers are carried on long stalks in March and April. Cultivation in clay pots is advisable, as is the use of loam-based compost in order to maintain the stability of the plant.

SHRUB-LIKE BEGONIAS

The majority of species and hybrids in this group are undoubtedly grown for their attractive and very varied foliage. This is an extremely large group of begonias numbering well over 300 registered cultivars and species, with untold unregistered varieties. The foliage of these plants varies from the bare-leaved types to those which are covered in fine hairs; from large to small leaves; with leaves of different shapes and textures. Most of the flowers are either white or pink, occasionally apricot, and their blooming period can effectively cover the entire year, although in general this is of secondary importance.

As the name implies these plants tend to be rather bushy, with lots of basal shoots produced during the main growing period. Given the right amount of heat, light and humidity, the plants in this group do not have a dormant period, though there is still a major growing season for all of them. During this growing period great efforts must be made to train and groom the plants. For those which tend to grow erect this means, in simple terms, pinching out growing tips to promote branching lower down, thus creating a bushier plant. Pruning means shortening the outer stems so that the final shape is a symmetrical dome.

The Shrub-like begonias like as high a light level as can be borne without causing leaf-scorch. In Britain, where most plants have to be grown under protection, this probably means without shading except at the height of the day – early morning and late afternoon sunlight will do no harm. Those with bare leaves will stand more sun than the hairy leaved types, but the best foliage with the best colour and the most prolific flowering can only be obtained with adequate light levels. Too high a light level results in foliage which is undersized and pale in colour, whereas too low a light level will produce dark-coloured foliage which is oversized.

Most Shrub-like begonias are not too selective about temperature, being prepared to grow anywhere with a range of 55–70°F (13–21°C), though 60°F (16°C) is best. Most will survive temperatures down to 45°F (7.5°C) though without any growth. Violent fluctuations in temperature can be a cause of leaf drop and unsatisfactory blooming. For the vast majority of this type of begonia atmospheric humidity is not a special problem, though they do prefer this to be above 40 per cent. However, there are a number of individual plants which will need to be grown in a terrarium to provide the necessary higher humidity.

Shrub-like begonias need to be fed throughout their growing period with a balanced fertilizer, watered in twice a week at half strength. Just prior to the flowering period this fertilizer can be changed to one which is higher in potash. No feeding is required during the period when growth is at a minimum.

From what has been said it is clear that these Shrub-like types can be grown successfully as houseplants. If there is a problem with them it is that the light values may be somewhat on the low side for the best results. This can be corrected by placing the plant in a well-lit window, avoiding only the high intensity of the midday sun.

As we have seen there is a large range of available species and cultivars in this group. Here we shall give a number of examples which are fairly easily obtained.

B. 'Argenteo-guttata'

A hybrid whose name means 'silver speckled', but which has been given the popular name, 'Trout Leaf'. The plant is a cross between a Cane-stemmed species *B. albo-picta* and a Thick-stemmed species *B. olbia*. The olive-green leaves are covered with silver spots, and the rose-pink flowers are produced in moderate quantity in spring and summer.

B. 'Burle Marx'

Now known to be a species imported from Brazil and more correctly named *B. glaziovii*. It is a small Shrub-like plant, which will eventually reach 2ft (60cm) across. The leaves, which are about 5in (13cm) across, are obovate in shape but with rather an angular look about them. They are green but with reddish patches between the veins. The most characteristic feature of the leaves is the pustular texture of the upper surface. Small clusters of white flowers are borne in spring and summer. This species is very easy to grow and will happily withstand temperatures down to about 40°F (4.5°C).

Though the usual propagation method for the Shrub-like begonias is by stem cuttings, *B. glaziovii*, *B. exotica* and *B. listida* are treated more like the Rhizomatous types, that is by leaf cuttings.

B. cubensis
A species from Cuba which, because of its leaves, is also known as 'Holly Leaf'. The drooping habit makes it very useful for a basket. The white flowers, flushed pink, are produced in the winter.

B. 'Digswelliana'
A hybrid between *B. fuchsiodes* and *B. semperflorens*, producing its bright red buds in the winter (the buds do not always open).

B. exotica
A species discovered in New Guinea 40 years ago, and which has quite unusual foliage. The large leaves are basically dark green but covered with pink/purplish patches between the veins. The margins are saw-toothed. The plant can attain 4ft (1.2m) in height, and the pink flowers are produced in late autumn.

B. fuchsiodes
A species from Mexico introduced 150 years ago with thick, small, shiny dark green leaves. The plant branches very easily and can easily become a bit of a mess. The flowering season can be anywhere from summer through to winter. (The tiny pink flowers are somewhat pendulous and reminiscent of a fuchsia.) The variety *miniata* is very similar except that the flowers are red. Though a valuable plant in its own right *B. fuchsiodes* has played an important role in the development of the Semperflorens group of begonias. If unsupported the stems can become pendent, thus making this species useful for growing in a basket.

B. incarnata
A species from Mexico which has upright stems which may attain a height of some 30in (76cm). The leaves are light green and ovate, the margins being slightly toothed and covered in fine hairs. The pale-pink flowers are produced in abundance during the winter months. This species, crossed with *B. nitida*, has the reputation of having produced the very first Shrub-like hybrid B. 'Ingramii', though in all fairness the precise parentage has been challenged.

B. listida

A Brazilian species which can reach a height of 12in (3.7cm). The shrubby plant is most attractive with long, narrow dark-green leaves, each having a distinct emerald green stripe along the main vein. The reverse of the leaves is blood red, and the white flowers are produced in the autumn/winter.

The emerald green stripe along the main vein is a characteristic handed on to a number of *B. listida* hybrids, for example 'Raymond George Nelson', 'Magdalene Madsen', 'Serlis', and 'Murray Morrison'.

B. luxurians

A Brazilian species introduced in 1848 and completely unlike the typical begonia. The large leaves resemble palm tree foliage, and in its natural habitat it can reach up to 8ft (2.4m) in height. In order to restrict their height in the greenhouse, and also to produce a more shapely plant, it is necessary to commence pinching out the growing tips whilst they are quite young. Grown properly this species will produce yellowish white fragrant flowers in the late summer. The author finds this species very prone to aphid attack over summer.

B. 'Medora'

A hybrid of unknown parentage which has 3in (7.5cm) long, narrow leaves, dark green, and covered in silver spots. The thin, cane-like stems grow to about 2½ft (76cm) and are covered with small, rose-pink flowers in the late autumn. A plain green leafed variety 'Green Medora', which has white flowers, has also been reported.

B. serratipetala

A species from New Guinea with bronze-coloured, highly serrated leaves which are marked with raised red/pink spots. The pink flowers are not profusely borne, and the plant needs plenty of light to help the production of bloom. This species is not the easiest to grow being somewhat sensitive to the amount of water given, too much or too little causing extensive leaf drop. It appears to do better when grown in the house.

B. 'Thurstonii'

A cross between *B. metallica* and *B. sanguinea* and one of the most popular Shrub-like varieties today. The mature plant can attain a height of some 3ft (90cm) and can become rather straggly unless

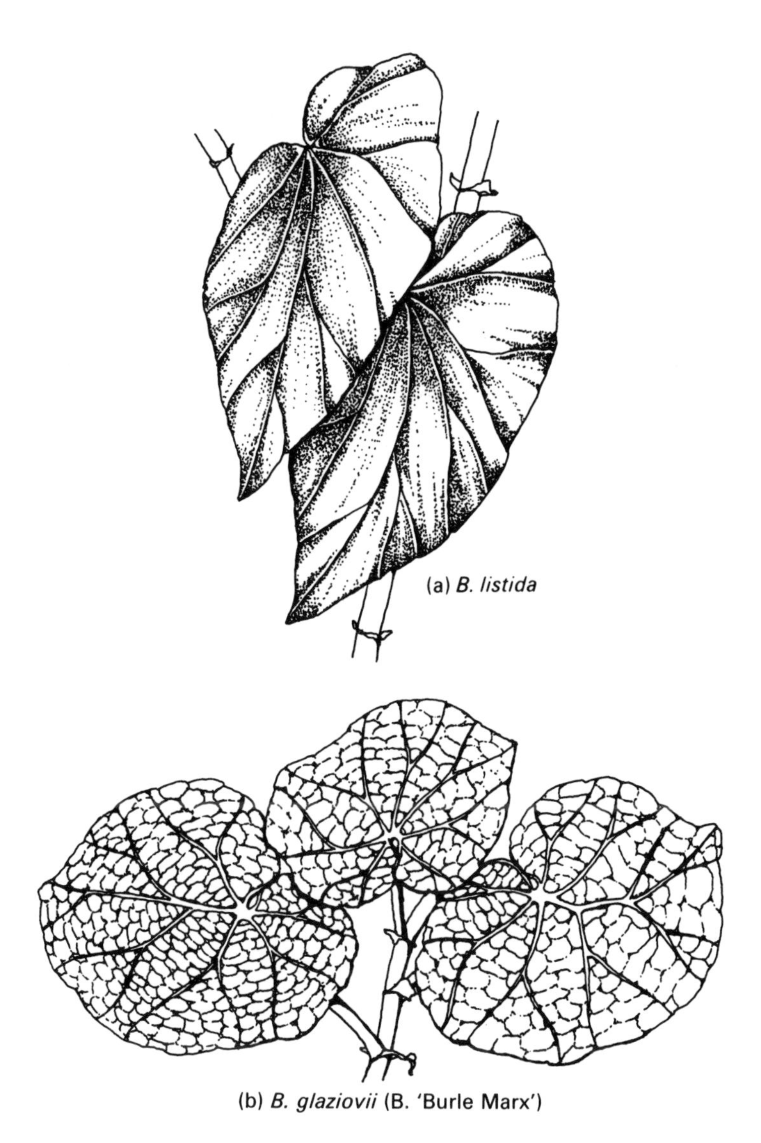

Shrub-like begonias: (a) the main vein areas are very pale in colour compared to the dark velvety green of the leaf surface; (b) the rather rectangular leaves are entirely deeply pustular.

kept well pruned and pinched. The upper surfaces of the leaves are a stunning, glossy, olive green, and the reverse is blood-red producing a remarkably attractive effect when the sunlight shines through the foliage. The stems are clothed in fine white hairs. The small pink flowers are bearded and appear in mid-summer.

All the Shrub-like begonias above are bare-leaved, but there are also the hairy-leaved types of which the following are merely examples:

B. kellermanii
A species introduced from Guatemala about 70 years ago. The thick, convex, green leaves are covered with a felt of white hairs. The white flowers, flushed pink, are produced in panicles during the very early spring. Very easily grown from seed.

B. metallica
A well-known species from Brazil which has small, dark green leaves with depressed purple veins. The whole surface is covered with fine, silver hairs. The pink flowers (also covered in pink hairs) are produced in the autumn. Stem cuttings need to be dry to root successfully.

B. scharffii
A species introduced from Brazil in 1888 has fairly broad leaves which are mid-green and covered in white hairs. Grown to maturity the plant can reach 3ft (90cm) in height and 2ft (60cm) across in a few years. The very pale-pink, hairy flowers are seen during the winter months.

B. venosa
Another Brazilian species. It has fairly large, succulent green leaves which are convex and covered with a felt-like mass of white hairs. Under the best conditions it can reach 3ft (90cm) in height. As with the species above it needs to be grown in as dry a condition as possible, and water must not splash the foliage. It does, however, appreciate full sun during the growing period. The bunches of white flowers seem to appear throughout the year.

The hybrids and species listed above represent but a very small percentage of those available today. On the whole they tend to be easy going in their growing requirements.

11
GROWING FOR SHOWING, AND JUDGING BEGONIAS

There is very little doubt that showing or exhibiting begonias, or any type of flower or vegetable, is not everyone's most favourite leisure activity. From the largest national societies down to the smallest local flower and vegetable club show, secretaries have the greatest difficulty in cajoling members into bringing exhibits to their annual show. Most members seem to gain satisfaction from growing plants to a reasonable standard, and from the camaraderie that membership brings.

Nevertheless, the showing of begonias is an opportunity to measure one's achievements against those of other growers, and in doing so to set standards which will spread throughout the entire begonia-growing fraternity. It is largely through the show bench that new varieties, both amateur and professional, are assessed, retained, or dispensed with. Of course the problem of showing begonias is that occasionally a new variety will be released which has a special quality (for example a new colour break), but lacking the size expected of a show variety people think it inferior when it most certainly is not. In other words too many people concentrate on begonias which regularly appear in the lists of prize winners, neglecting a vast number of plants, and causing them eventually to disappear. And that is undoubtedly sad and wrong. Certainly in the case of large-flowered Tuberous double begonias, a number of most attractive varieties have all but disappeared from cultivation because of the negative influence of show results. In this respect one thinks of the lovely picotee/bicolour 'Saturn', and the almost perfectly formed pink 'Jean Paddon Smith', amongst many others.

Nonetheless, there are many growers who, bitten by the show bug, will always wish to show their plants and blooms, and this chapter is intended for those who want to pursue this aim.

In Britain there are six or seven shows in which quite large sections are entirely devoted to begonias, together with a further half-dozen in which begonias play an important role. In all these shows, however, by far the greatest emphasis is placed on classes for the large-flowered Tuberous, double hybrids (Non-tuberous begonias playing a very minor role). Indeed, in those shows where such plants can be exhibited the schedule usually restricts the classes to '. . . begonias other than Tuberous doubles'. The consequence is that, in such classes, a Cane-stemmed plant might be in competition with perhaps a Semperflorens or a Rhizomatous plant. This is a most unsatisfactory state of affairs, and one must go to America or Australia to see classes for competition between plants from the same specific begonia grouping. Efforts are being made in Britain to encourage the showing of Non-tuberous begonias, but the prospects do not appear good.

Since Tuberous begonias are treated almost as though they were annual plants it is the normal practice to grow specific varieties for a particular show. Consequently the timing of blooms assumes a significant part of the cultivation. Growing for showing is a much more positive activity where Tuberous begonias are concerned than for many of the other types discussed in this book. Most of this chapter, therefore, will be devoted to the cultivation of Tuberous begonias for showing, and that includes their transportation, staging and judging, with a few comments on the Non-tuberous types.

At the dozen or so major begonia shows in Britain each year classes are of two types, pot plants and cut blooms. These two types of classes can be further sub divided as follows.

PLANTS IN POTS

Group Displays: Usually to cover a given area of, say, 8ft (2.4m) wide × 4ft (1.2m) deep. This type of exhibit is also usually restricted as to its height, for example 6ft (1.8m) or 8ft (2.4m). The number of plants required could vary from 25 to perhaps 40, depending upon the type of plant grown. It is normal for such a display to include foliage material, such as ferns, and might even permit the use of other begonias, such as Pendulas or Rexes, but only 'to finish off the display'.

A Group of Large-Flowered, Tuberous, Double Begonias: Again, occupying a given space perhaps 6ft (1.8m) × 4ft (1.2m), but here allowing only fern-like plants to be used and no other begonias. Also, the total number of pots might be restricted, perhaps not more than 20, and in restricted choice, for example not less than three distinct varieties.

(Both of the above classes will also include the phrase '. . . to be arranged for effect . . .', which means that the judges will consider not only the individual quality of the plants but they will also take into account the way in which they have been arranged.)

Pot Plants: These may be either single pot plants or multiple pots (with three, six, nine or twelve). In the multiple pot classes there may also be some restriction as to varieties, for example . . . 'three pots in at least two varieties . . .'. Other than this restriction they may be grown as and how one wishes.

Restricted Pot Plants: These are pot plants which have to be grown in pots of restricted size, usually a maximum of 7in (18cm) in diameter, and which are also restricted in the type of growth – for example one main stem with not more than three flowering side shoots, each on the main stem.

Single-Stem Plants: A class peculiar to Scotland in which the plant is grown as one main stem with all side shoots removed.

Pendulas and Cascades: Usually referred to as 'hanging baskets'. This is the only class for Tuberous begonias which permits growing more than one tuber in a container.

CUT BLOOMS

As far as the author is aware Britain is the only country where it is possible to show the cut bloom heads of Tuberous begonias. These classes were originally introduced to enable growers who had considerable distances to travel to compete in shows without having to overcome the problem of transporting entire plants. Today, of course, there are amateur hybridists who are developing new varieties largely on the basis of their potential as producers of single blooms. The cut bloom classes are further divided as follows.

Single-Cut Blooms: A class intended for novices only.

Multi-Cut Bloom Classes: Usually three and six cut blooms, often with a restriction in terms of varieties. In the major shows there will also be 'colour classes' where there will be a restriction in terms of colour; for instance three cut blooms in orange or yellow, or three cut blooms in pink or salmon, or three cut blooms in three distinct cultivars. It is only in these cut bloom classes that provision is made to separate picotee or bicolours into groups, to the exclusion of self-colours. The ultimate challenge in cut bloom cultivation, for instance twelve cut blooms, is to be found in only the two Society National Shows (where they are Championship classes), plus one other show.

Once again, it is only in the larger shows that one sometimes finds classes in which one plant, together with a cut bloom (always the same variety), are called for. In Britain at the present there is little opportunity for the growers of the other types of plant described in this book to compete, which is an unfortunate situation.

As was stated in the introduction, the techniques described here are the results of many discussions with many successful enthusiasts. Among them are those who believe that it is possible to reduce successful cultivation to a scientific operation, but that simply cannot be true. In so many instances those growers who have continued success on the show bench really do not know how exactly they do it. They seem to possess an inner knowledge and 'feel' for plants that defies quantifying. It might be possible for them to pass on their knowledge by example, but they will not be able to provide continuous contact and instruction over the entire growing period. The best that can be done here is to distil such information so that the basic principles are conveyed. Thereafter, readers must develop their own 'version'.

When talking to successful exhibitors one fact that is immediately evident is their single-minded approach to a particular show. Planning takes place when the begonias are brought into growth, if not even earlier. Drawing up a 'battle plan' is an important part of the showman's year.

The first step, after targeting a number of shows, is to determine what one intends to show. Will it be plants, and in a group? Are they to be shown as pot plants, or grown in restricted size pots? If it is to be pot plants, then do you have the appropriate varieties? It is well to remember that certain varieties of Tuberous begonia produce very few side shoots, or perhaps flower stems which do not elongate sufficiently to lift the flower heads clear of the foliage, or produce an excessive amount of foliage, or tend to be very tall growers. With those factors in mind a short list of varieties can be selected by colour, from which one can make a final choice. They are, for pot plants:

White: 'Avalanche', 'Billie Langdon'.
Pink: 'Sweet Dreams', 'Krakatoa', 'Melissa', 'Sugar Candy'.
Red: 'Linda Jackson', 'Sultan', 'Royalty'.
Yellow: 'Midas' (foliage needs reducing), 'Joburg'.
Picotee/bicolour: 'Fred Martin', 'Fairylight', 'Masquerade'.
Orange/apricot: 'Tahiti', 'Apricot Delight', 'Suzanne Redmayne', 'City of Ballaarat'.

This is a useful, but by no means complete list. If, on the other hand, the intention is to grow cut blooms then a slightly different selection is required.

White: 'Bernat Klein', 'Avalanche', 'Alice Gold' (in Scotland this variety would be acceptable as a yellow).
Pink: 'Sweet Dreams', 'Falstaff', 'Roy Hartley', 'Gypsy'
Red: 'Linda Jackson', 'Red Velvet', 'Goliath', 'Red Admiral', 'Tom Brownlee'.
Yellow: 'Joburg', 'Midas'.
Picotee/bicolour: 'Gay Gordon', 'Fred Martin', 'Jessie Cruickshank', 'Fairylight', 'Golden Bali Hi'.
Orange/apricot: 'Tahiti', 'Apricot Delight', 'Suzanne Redmayne', 'City of Ballaarat'.

I should stress that this list is my own personal starting point, and that while clearly some varieties can serve both purposes, one plant cannot!

Having selected the type of classes to enter, and the likely varieties, you should now peruse the show schedules from the previous year to determine the possibilities available. (And, to be on the safe side, ring the various secretaries to enquire whether there have been any changes in the past year.) Some shows do not draw any distinction between novices and more experienced growers, but the schedule of classes will make this clear. Usually, the definition of a novice is someone who has not won a first prize in any begonia show.

In the annual show of The National Begonia Society, apart from novice classes there are also classes for growers of intermediate ability before they progress to the senior or open classes. The final piece of information to note is the likely date of the show, indicating when the begonias must be started into growth so that they are at their flowering peak at the right time (that is with five or six leaves per main stem). For example, the major period for the larger begonia shows is from the beginning of August to the first weekend in September, no more than five weeks at the most. If the show is in early August then a late March start is soon enough, whereas if the show is in early September then mid- to late April will be satisfactory.

Once you have decided first, whether you are going to grow plants, how many, for what purpose and what varieties, and second, whether you are going to grow for cut blooms, how many and in what classes, comes the next question. Are all tubers of any one variety equally suitable for both these purposes? By and large the answer has to be no, though it is not always possible to realize the ideal situation. Generally speaking, if intending to grow cut blooms, or for a group class, or plants in restricted pots, then an approximately three-year-old tuber is about the best to use. However, if the intention is to grow pot plants for unrestricted single and multi-pot classes, then the larger (or older) the tuber is the better. For the latter classes the intention is to develop no less than four main stems per plant, and the older tubers will be capable of doing this rather than the younger ones. Of course in practice there will always be the odd tuber which breaks this rule, but by and large it is the one to follow.

In the early stages of cultivation the treatment of all the tubers will be exactly the same. Different approaches commence from mid-season onwards. It cannot be stressed too much that the factor which matters most in the growing of show plants is that of consistency throughout the whole season, and without this it is hardly worth starting.

CULTIVATION

After thoroughly inspecting the selected tubers for any signs of rot they are placed on a bed of damp compost, whereupon more is added so that the crowns are then about ½in (13mm) below the surface. The ideal containers for this exercise are 4in (10cm) deep plastic trays, with sufficient drainage holes in the base. The trays are then placed on a heated sand bed so that the base temperature is thermostatted at approximately 75°F (24°C). It will take some 24 hours before the temperature in the tray will properly stabilize, but when it does it needs to be about 70°F (21°C). This temperature should be properly checked using a thermometer which is capable of indicating the correct temperature.

This is extremely important and to underline this point I have checked four different horticultural thermometers against a scientific standard, and found two to be about 2°F (0.5°C) higher, but one read no less than 11°F (6.5°C) higher than the true value! Of course this is far better than being 11°F lower than the true value, but it does leave a lot to be desired. A sheet of clear glass over the tray will help to retain moisture in the compost.

The compost chosen should be the peat-based type as described in Chapter 15, either home-produced or purchased from a reputable supplier. The compost should have an adequate air-filled porosity of between 15 and 20 per cent, and usually any correction to the commercially available materials involves adding coarse sand. While checking the porosity the pH of the compost should also be measured, and the easiest way is by using test papers obtained at the larger chemists. As an alternative, use the soil test kits now readily available at most garden centres. If the deviation from pH 6.5 is greater than about 0.5 units, you must correct the balance.

Not all the tubers in the trays will start into growth at the same time, but growing points should be showing after three to four weeks. During this time the compost should be examined daily to ensure that it is not drying out at the base of the tray, and water will need to be sprayed over the compost almost on a daily basis to maintain an adequate moisture level. As soon as the growing tips break through the surface of the compost the glass should be removed to avoid droplets of water falling on to them, and possibly leading to rot.

From now on the compost must be kept uniformly moist throughout its depth to encourage the maximum root growth. If root growth goes to plan then within a very short time there will be a considerable amount of entanglement between neighbouring tubers. This will make it impossible to remove individual tubers without causing considerable damage to the root system(s), and thereby subjecting the growing plants to a serious check in their development. That being the case the tubers should be given plenty of room when they are first placed in the trays, at least 2in (5cm) around each one. To avoid this entanglement it is helpful to surround the tuber, and its 2in (5cm) of compost, with a strip of polythene film of the same width as the depth of the container. The roots will grow out as far as the polythene barrier.

The treatment given to the tubers during their first few weeks in the trays will be determined greatly by the experience of previous

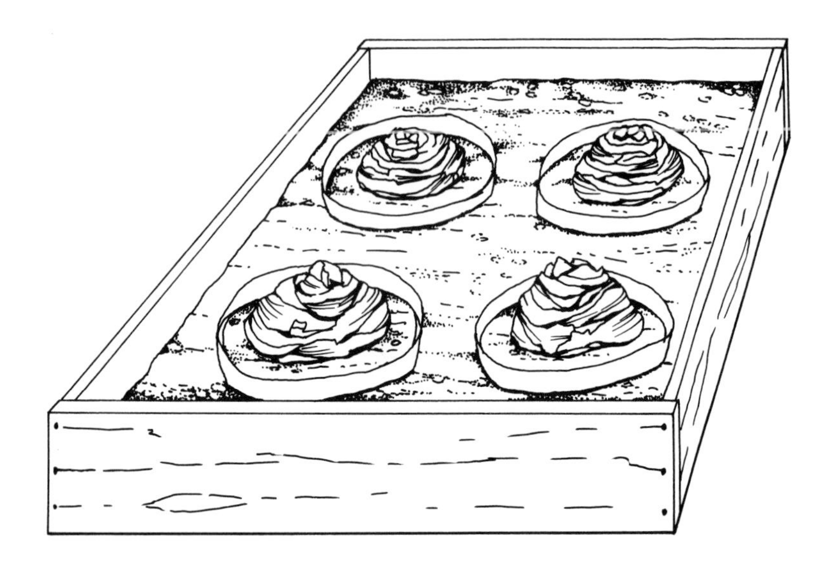

The tubers should be encircled by a strip of polythene film to help confine the developing roots.

years. For example, my own experience has been that fungal growths can appear on the surface of the compost causing emerging shoots from the tubers to be infected. Mixing Benlate into the water has effectively prevented these attacks. It also appears that the use of Benlate keeps begonia mite at bay at this stage of growth.

When the growths are from 1½–2in (4–5cm) high, the tuber should be carefully eased from the compost to examine the developing root system. Remember that at this stage it is the root development which is all-important. When the root ball can almost fill the palm of the hand, the plant is removed from the heated bed and potted into a pot of the correct size. Of course the root ball will be proportionately larger with the older and bigger tubers.

With modern-day composts with the correct, air-filled porosity there is no need to pot on later in the season into larger sized pots. The first potting needs to be the only one. For the cut bloom plants, those intended for group displays, and those for restricted pot size classes, a two- or three-year-old tuber should have developed sufficient root to require a container of 7in (18cm) diameter. However, for the individual pot plants the older tubers (that is 3 years) might need pots up to 12in (30cm) in diameter.

The plants are placed in the pots so that the top of the tuber is some 2–2½in (5–6.5cm) below the top rim, allowing for top-dressing later in the season. The compost should be moist to the point where it just clings together when squeezed in the hand. If, in the past, your begonias have been troubled by the attentions of vine weevil then it would be sensible to incorporate a small amount of gamma-HCH, about 1 teaspoon per bushel (35l), into the compost at this stage. After potting, the plants should be placed on the bench out of direct sunlight but in a well-lit position. From now on it is essential that the greenhouse temperature should not be allowed to fall below 60°F (16°C), and should preferably be kept to 65–70°F (18.5–21°C).

Up to about May you should provide a restricted amount of heat overnight, but this should be kept to an absolute minimum. All that is necessary is that the plants should be kept growing at all times – continuous, consistent growth is what is necessary. During daylight hours the probability is that the temperature will rise well above 70°F (21°C), and plenty of ventilation will be required on most days. As the season progresses into May and June so the daytime temperatures will rise sharply and the greenhouse humidity will fall. To maintain a humidity of about 80 per cent it will be necessary to put a lot of moisture into the atmosphere. This is best carried out using the low-volume, multi-headed sprayers which produce a fog-like supply of water over the plants. Alternatively (and far less satisfactorily), spread copious amounts of water over the floor.

It is precisely at this stage of growth, during May and June, that begonia mite is at its most active. Low greenhouse humidity encourages the attentions of this pest, and anything that you can do to discourage an attack of mite is to the good. In Australia, where the climate is much more arid than here in Britain, one of the treatments against the mite involves spraying with wettable sulphur. (At one time this was the recommended treatment against red spider mite and gall mite in blackcurrants.) As far as I am aware wettable sulphur is no longer available in Britain, and the only acaricide to recommend is derris. However, it is known that some fungicides are effective against mites, so spraying with Benomyl may very well work against this pest. A possible alternative would be a bio-friendly insecticidal soap which should be used in low concentration. If you have had a previous experience of begonia mite attack then an early preventative spray could help to keep this pest at bay.

WATERING AND FEEDING

Three possible methods of deciding when a pot needs water can be tried. First, test the weight of the pot in the hand. After a little practice you can usually decide when water is required. Second, scrape away the top 1in (2.5cm) of compost to determine the degree of dryness. And third, use a moisture meter which can be notoriously unreliable, unless it is a good meter used properly.

Once again the objective is to maintain adequate moisture in the compost, and also to ensure that there is a sufficient supply of air to maintain bacterial activity in the medium.

No matter how careful you are when potting up, some of the roots will become damaged and the plant will suffer considerable stress in the process. In addition, at this time of the year, evaporation and transpiration rates will be low and so watering, and therefore feeding, will be infrequent. For these reasons it will be necessary to foliar feed daily, unless the weather is dull. The humid, buoyant atmosphere will ensure that the leaf surfaces are readily penetrated by these feeds. Rapid penetration will also be assisted by adding a small amount of spreading agent to the feed. Since there is adequate phosphate in the compost a commercial foliar feed of NPK 26:0:26, diluted to one-quarter strength, will be ideal. Alternatively, a suitable foliar feed can be made up to one or other of the following formulations, using readily available materials.

Urea ½lb (0.2kg)		Ammonium nitrate ½lb (0.2kg)
Nitrate of potash ½lb (0.2kg)	or	Nitrate of potash ½lb (0.2kg)

Dissolve the mix in 2gl (9l) of water, whereupon 30ml (1fl.oz) of this master solution is diluted with 2gl (9l) of water to give the spray solution.

After about two weeks a stake is inserted into the compost behind each of the main stems, the intention being to provide support later in the season. From this point on cultivation is largely a question of keeping a watchful eye on the watering, foliar feeding, maintaining the correct greenhouse humidity and temperature, shading the plants from direct sunlight and removing all buds.

FLOWER QUALITY

Where the plants are intended for cut bloom use, restricted pot size work or group display, then the development of only one main stem should be allowed. All extra shoots which develop from the tuber should be removed when they are about 2in (5cm) high and used as propagating material.

When side shoots develop they should be treated in a manner demanded by the ultimate use of the plant. Plants for cut blooms should have all side shoots removed when they are some 3in (7.5cm) long, and be used as stem cuttings or alternatively, if they are not required for cuttings, left on the plant with their growing tips removed. In this way they will remain to assist in the photosynthesis processes required of the plant. Plants intended for use in group displays may have the lower two side shoots left on to develop into bloom carrying shoots, but all others higher up the plant should be removed or have their tips pinched out. Those plants destined for restricted pot classes will be allowed to keep the side shoots permitted by the show schedule, but in this instance it would be better to remove all side shoots in excess of this number.

The older and larger plants intended for the pot plant classes will have to be treated quite differently. First of all one must realize that as soon as the number of main stems exceeds one, then it is necessary to take into account the direction in which the blooms will face when the plant is in full flower. In general, begonia blooms tend to face in the direction taken by the leaf tips on the flowering stem. So, for instance, the flowers from two main stems could face in either the same or opposite directions. The situation becomes more complex as the number of main stems increases.

Since we have suggested that a plant intended as an unrestricted pot plant should carry no less than four main stems, then at the extreme ends of the spectrum of bloom disposition one could have a plant in which all blooms pointed in one direction within an arc of say 140° (a forward-facing plant), or all facing outwards (an all-round plant). Unless the show schedule states otherwise (as, for example, in certain table classes in the annual show of the Scottish Begonia Society), then the judges are required to treat both types of plant in exactly the same way giving advantage to neither one nor the other. Speaking entirely personally it is my opinion that a pot plant should be properly balanced both in terms of the ratio of flower to foliage, and in respect of the distribution of blooms, and therefore my contention is that the flowers should be all around the

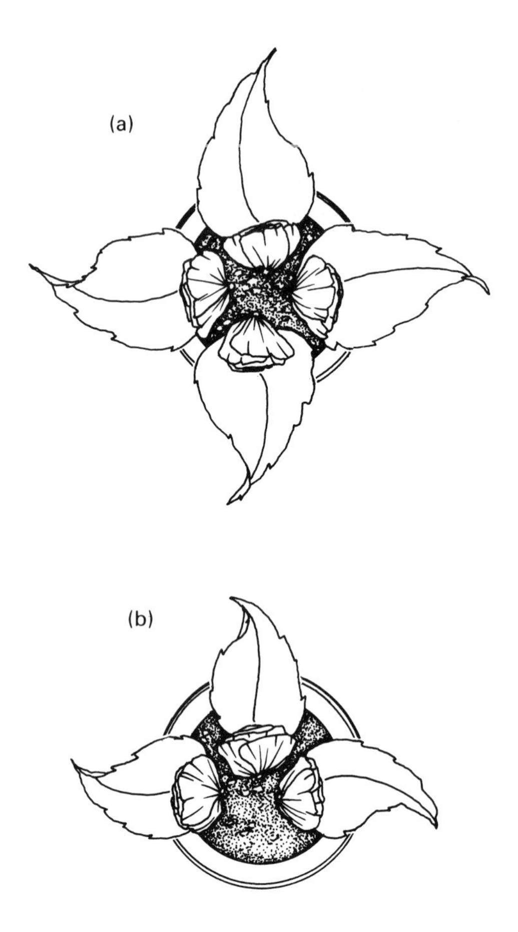

Styles of pot plant: (a) flowers facing forward; (b) flowers all around.

pot. Whether the plant is grown as an all-round or a forward-facing example (with the possible exception described), is a matter for the exhibitor to decide, but certainly any stems which face inwards should be removed as soon as possible.

At this stage of the season all buds must be removed when they are large enough to be pinched out without causing any damage to the growing point. The plants must be kept growing without any interruption, particular attention being constantly given to the state of the compost and its need for water. If the compost used has the correct air-filled porosity then it should be virtually impossible to overwater.

In the weeks that follow a constant check must be kept on the ties securing the main stems to the support stakes. The main stems increase quite rapidly in diameter and will require loosening fairly frequently if damage is to be avoided. In addition, where the larger plants are concerned it is sometimes necessary to use smaller supports for the side shoots which, under the best conditions, become quite substantial.

This treatment will continue until sometime in June when you have to think in terms of the forthcoming show, and of timing bud development so that they attain their maximum potential as blooms at just the right time. In principle it takes a bud of 1⅛in (3cm) diameter from five to seven weeks to attain maximum bloom size, depending upon the variety and, to a lesser extent, the weather conditions. There is also some evidence that the precise timing of a particular variety will depend on the specific location of the grower – latitude and altitude. Each individual grower must therefore determine the timings for varieties intended for the show bench. As a guideline only the timings for one or two varieties are:

'Fairylight'	38 days	'Roy Hartley'	42–49 days
'Sweet Dreams'	42 days	'City of Ballaarat'	42 days
'Red Admiral'	30 days	'Full Moon'	38 days

When in doubt work to an average figure of 42 days. Where cut blooms are concerned it is of some considerable advantage to 'bracket' the timings for any one variety, by which I mean to time one bloom say three days early, one three days late, and a third for the actual show date. Of course this procedure greatly increases the number of blooms required to be grown for any one show, but it does illustrate the extent to which some growers are prepared to go to win. There is also some evidence that where pot plants are concerned these timings can be shortened to some advantage.

With these timings in mind then, all buds of a size greater than the 1⅛in (3cm) diameter should be removed as carefully as possible, avoiding any damage to the growing point. This will leave probably one smaller bud following on behind that chosen to produce the show bloom, and this should also be left on the plant at this stage. After about two weeks the growing points should then be removed from every stem and side shoot, so allowing the vigour of the plant to be channelled into the growing bud(s).

At this stage it is also advisable to stop all foliar feeding to avoid any possible spotting of the flowers, and for the same reason the atmospheric humidity would be better reduced to around 50 per cent. Damping down should be more carefully controlled and must certainly not be done in the late afternoon. Any pest or disease problem cannot now be treated with sprays, but by the use of dry powders or smokes. Fortunately the only problems likely to be encountered are thrip (flower), caterpillars or earwigs, against which derris dust and permethrin smokes should provide adequate control.

As the buds develop it will be observed that on either side of the centre and male bud there is a flanking bud, which can be male or female. These flanking buds should be removed as soon as possible, without touching the central male bud. There is an opinion (as yet unproven) that the removal of these flanking buds will result in the centre one growing to a larger size. What is certain, however, is that as the buds grow the petals of the central male will eventually come into contact with those of the flanking buds. This can cause marking in the fully open flower, but also occasionally a slight deformation of the show bloom.

Removal of female buds. The two flanking buds must be carefully removed to allow undisturbed growth of centre and male bud.

To the best of the author's knowledge there is no rule which states that there is any requirement to remove these flanking buds, though in England it has become customary to do this. With regard to cut bloom cultivation, it is the desire to get a perfect single bloom which determines the need to remove the flanking buds.

It is at this stage that an increasing number of growers of cut blooms now place a flat disc or collar behind the growing bud. This circular disc measuring some 9in (23cm) in diameter may be cut from stiff cardboard, or better still from the lightweight, twin-wall polycarbonate plastic insulating material currently on the market. A ½in (13mm) wide slot cut from the centre to the circumference allows the disc to be slipped over the flower stem and behind the bud.

The idea is to persuade the developing back petals to remain flat, and not curl backwards as they tend to do on certain varieties. The other advantage is that the disc allows one to estimate quite accurately the size of the bloom. This practice is by no means universal, other growers preferring to avoid those varieties which have a tendency for the back petals to curl.

When cultivating for cut blooms, note that as the buds increase in size they will begin to touch the leaves. If allowed to continue this could mark the petals of the opening bud. At this point, therefore, the leaves are moved out of the way, twisting one leaf behind another where possible or, as a last resort, removing an offending leaf altogether. The objective is to allow the bud to develop freely and unrestricted.

Where pot plants are concerned problems do occasionally arise with those which are at the front of the benches, with their blooms extending far enough to restrict freedom of movement along the walkways. To avoid damage to the blooms as you brush against them, it is sometimes prudent to turn the pots so that their blooms face inwards and away from the pathway.

Feeding will now be required up to and beyond the show date, and once again almost every showperson has a specific recipe to give the best results. Many growers find, however, that feeding with Phostrogen (NPK 10:10:27), or any other fertilizer of similar composition at one-quarter strength and at three in every four waterings, is quite satisfactory. The fourth watering is with pure water to wash through any build up in deleterious salts. In the two weeks before the show two treatments with a solution of monoammonium phosphate – ¼ teaspoon per 1gl (4.5l) can also help to improve bloom size.

Whether or not this 'bloom feed' is at all effective is a debatable point, but it is a fact that the longer the bud is in growth before opening the larger the bloom is likely to be. Good light, coupled with low temperatures, seem to help delaying the bud opening sufficiently to allow maximum petal growth.

You may recall that when the buds were being 'taken' for the show blooms, we referred to another, smaller one, following on. Where pot plants are concerned these small buds can and should be left on the plant, but opinion is divided where cut blooms are concerned. Some very eminent cut bloom growers leave these small buds in place and use them quite successfully as cut blooms for later shows, whilst other and equally expert cut bloom growers prefer to remove them seven days after securing the show bud.

It is well to appreciate that all these show plants, having been 'stopped', will not produce any further blooms but they might well provide a second crop of late basal cuttings.

MISCELLANEOUS BEGONIAS

Apart from the Tuberous types most other begonias are not treated as annual plants, and so the preparation for a show involves, in one sense, growing them to the best of one's ability year in and year out. For example, where the Cane-stemmed and the Shrub-like begonias are concerned this means keeping them well groomed and well trimmed for an attractive shape. It also means continually removing debris, keeping pests at bay, staking and training stems, repotting regularly, maintaining a fresh, lively look to the foliage, and above all keeping it clean. The effects of pests are particularly worrying where the damage is still evident the following year.

TRANSPORTATION

There seems little point in expending so much time and effort coaxing the plants to produce perfect blooms at the right time, simply to undo all that work by careless transportation to the show site. Begonia blooms do bruise fairly easily, and the red ones in particular.

The cut blooms are carried in deep cardboard boxes, those known as 'turkey boxes' being especially suitable since they are usefully deep at about 12in (30cm). Most exhibitors seem to cut their blooms between 10pm on the eve and 5am on the morning of the show, and insist that this is an important factor in ensuring that the blooms are at their best at judging time. The flower stem is cut as long as possible and then carefully inserted through the rubber cap of an orchid bloom tube, which contains water or some other suitable liquid, or alternatively it is wrapped in a small piece of wet cotton wool. Then a 2in (5cm) deep layer of cotton wool or wood wool is laid in the bottom of the box, and the blooms are placed on horseshoe collars of the same material so that the back petals rest flat on the collars. The flower stems are then taped down to the cotton wool, or even the base of the box, using a suitable transparent adhesive tape.

Depending on the size of blooms, the size of box and the care which one wishes to display, it should be possible to carry between six and eight blooms per box. The lid is replaced after making certain that it does not touch the blooms at any point, and the box is now ready for transporting. It should be possible to get up to two such boxes into the boot of a family-size car. It is a good idea to consider the possible combinations of cut blooms to be used in the show before packing the boxes, so that all those for one exhibit finish up in the same box. This helps overcome the utter confusion which always seems to reign at staging time.

A timely word of warning must be given here: it is unwise to carry the bloom boxes on a car roof-rack for two reasons. First, the severe cooling effect of the air passing over the box can cause condensation of water vapour, with water droplets forming on the petals and marking them. And second, the pressure of the moving air can be quite considerable. One keen showman known to the author had the misfortune to have his prize blooms spread over a wide area of a motorway.

The transportation of plants is a much more difficult exercise, and one which dissuades many people from showing this type of exhibit. Certainly much greater care is required if the plants are to arrive at the show in a satisfactory condition. Since there is a tendency for flowering plants to be somewhat top-heavy some method of preventing them from falling over has to be found. Several techniques have been described and they illustrate the ingenuity of growers in overcoming the problem. It is important to realize, however, that though plants grown in pots of restricted size may be transported in a private vehicle, it really needs to be a station wagon (or similar), while a van is necessary for other plants.

Here are five methods which have been used. First, pots can be placed on the floor of a van with other inverted pots, or even bricks, wedged between them. This is not a highly successful method, but with care it can work if the distance travelled is not too great and the road surface not too bad. Second, pots can be buried up to the rim in boxes of sand. This can be very successful, but note that the sand might be too heavy a weight for the average car.

The third method involves constructing a wooden carrying

'cross'. Six pieces of timber 1⅜in (35mm) × ⅜in (10mm) are required, and cut to the following sizes:

1 × 14½in (36cm)	2 × 4¾in (11.5cm)
2 × 6¾in (17.5cm)	1 × 10¾in (26.5cm)

Two sections are constructed from the above pieces using panel pins. The pot is placed on the centre of the cross and strong twine is used between points A & C, and B & D. Since the arms of the cross are longer than the pot diameter the whole structure becomes quite stable.

The penultimate method involves concrete blocks cast in a rectangular box 4in (10cm) deep. When making supports for 7in (18cm) diameter pots, the box should be about 12in (30cm) square. Before filling with wet concrete a 7in (18cm) pot is placed in the box so that, on setting, a circular hole is produced in the centre of the concrete block.

The fifth and final method involves a pot-plant carrier (resembling a mediaeval punishment stocks) made in timber and designed to fit the boot of a hatchback car (the outside dimensions will have to depend on the make and model). This carrier, made by Mr Gammon of Barnstaple, England, is a good illustration of the lengths some exhibitors will go to when transporting their plants safely.

Whatever the method selected to transport the plants the blooms will still need to be covered with cotton wool or wood wool, loosely draped over the face of the flowers, so that they do not get damaged. Cotton wool needs to be placed between the petals and any adjacent leaves to prevent chafing. The main stems need to be firmly fastened to the stakes, but the bloom supports must be slightly slackened to allow for a little movement of the flower stems otherwise they could break.

STAGING

On arriving at the showground you should find out exactly where your plants or blooms have to be staged, and whether everything necessary for the staging is readily available. There is nothing more disturbing for an exhibitor who is intending to set up a group, and who unloads all the plants, than when he discovers that the staging has not yet been erected, or that the group is to be staged in another place.

If everything is ready for the exhibits then all plants and blooms

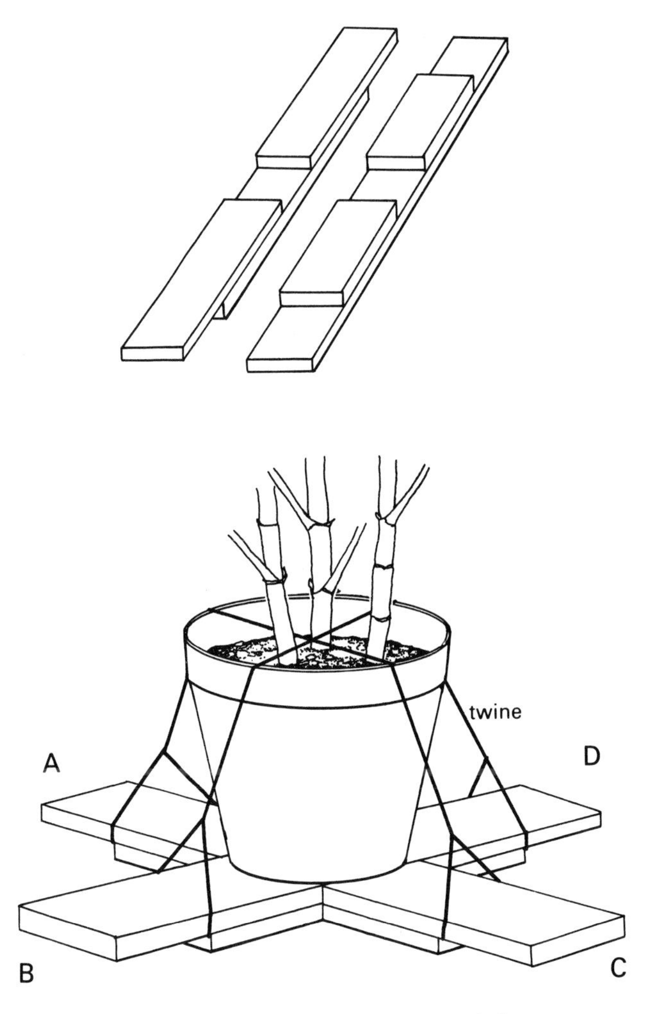

Securing pot plants for transportation. A simple home-made device which will stabilize the pots when placed on a flat surface.

can be moved close to where they will be staged. A table on which to place the plant material prior to staging is always very useful, but not always available. Location of a water supply point is desirable, especially for the pot plants. A container for used plant material is also useful since it helps keep the show area fairly free of the inevitable debris. And finally, you should ensure that you have remembered to bring the class entry cards properly completed, and suitable plant and bloom identity labels. The staging can now begin.

The following is intended merely as a guideline for novice growers, the more experienced showpeople having already devised their own approach to staging. Where relevant it also represents my own personal thoughts rather than any established principles, or the rules of any society.

Group Classes

For most shows the staging for group classes will be provided by the show organisers, and consists of a number (usually three) of tiers or shelves 12in (30cm) deep and 12in high, and the full width of the exhibit as stated in the schedule. The staging tends to be covered in black drape, set against a black backcloth.

It helps if you now visualized the staging as being divided by an imaginary line running down the centre from top to bottom, and across the centre from left to right. The objective is to produce the effect of a slight mound in the centre of the exhibit from top to bottom and from left to right. The first plant to place on the staging goes in the centre of the back row, and should be a strong colour – red or orange – to focus the attention on the centre of the display, while also giving the exhibit height. Indeed this plant should stand about 4in (10cm) higher than either of its two neighbours.

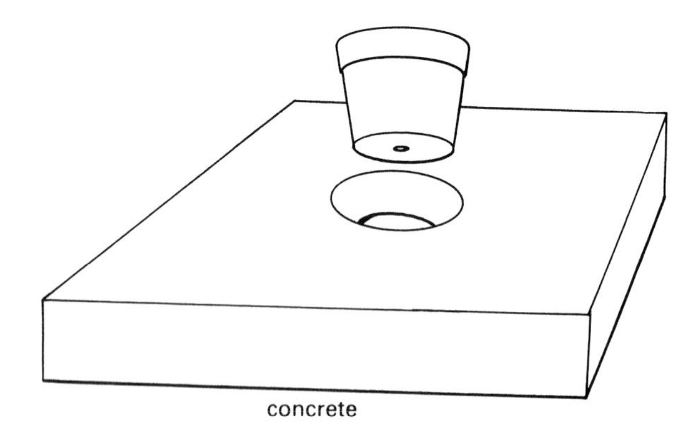

Transporting pot plants. Wet concrete is poured into a shallow tray, which contains a shallow pot of the correct size. The pot is removed before the concrete hardens.

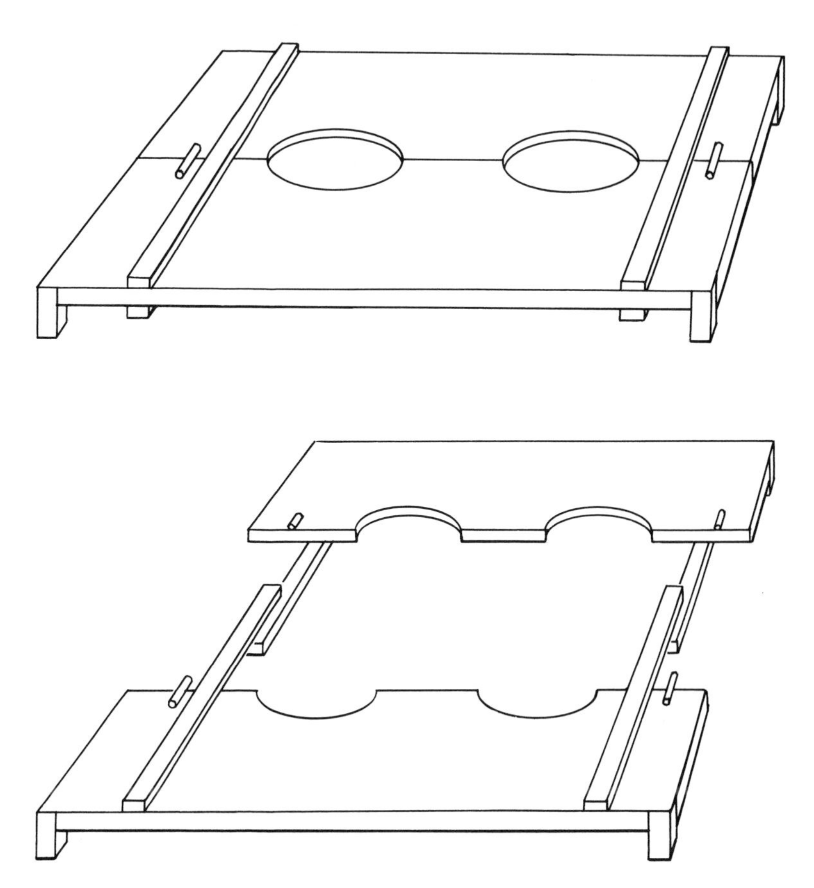

Supports for pots. A timber structure which can be made to fit a car boot and which will carry two plants.

The plants are now separated into colours so that whatever is placed on one side of the top-to-bottom dividing line can be balanced by identical (or very similar colours) on the other side. The stronger colours occupy the centre line, becoming gradually weaker as you proceed to the left and right edges. Also note that you should avoid using a very deep-red (crimson) plant since it tends to create a 'hole' in the exhibit.

The gaps between pots can now be filled in, with the bare pots being hidden by the use of maidenhair or asparagus fern, or even bracken fronds. These ferns additionally play a useful part in softening the outlines between plants. Pots of Jacaranda (grown from seed) make an attractive foil for Tuberous begonias exhibited as a group display. Meanwhile, if you do not want the array of exposed pots to be seen, cover them with a piece of black cloth. The exhibitor should remember to water all the pots before staging, and to lift the blooms carefully so that they face the judges.

All plants should be labelled either with the varietal name, or with the word 'seedling' printed clearly in black ink on a small white card. The card should be placed in the pot on a piece of split cane, set low down so that it can be read easily without being obtrusive. Judges do not particularly like labels stuck on leaves, or pinned to the foliage, or even towering above the plant.

The schedules describing group classes should be read very carefully since they often contain small-print restrictions which have led over the years to the occasional 'Not According to Schedule (NAS)' verdict. To illustrate this point it is worth comparing the schedule for the group class at a local British (Southport) show, and the National Show. The schedule in the former says, 'Group of Large-Flowered, Tuberous, Double Begonias in Pots' in bloom, and not more than 20 pots. In this instance no hanging baskets or Pendula begonias are allowed. On the other hand, the schedule for the National Show requires 'Group of Tuberous, Double Begonias in Pots, Hanging Baskets etc.' In addition, the former show schedule states quite clearly that foliage material may be used but not Non-tuberous begonias, whereas the National Show schedule does permit the use of say, Rhizomatous or Rex begonias since they are classed as foliage plants.

A recent incident illustrates the problems schedules can cause the judges. An exhibitor at the National Show finished off the front of his group exhibit with some very attractive Rieger begonias. The judges allowed the exhibit even though it was clearly NAS since the Rieger plants are neither truly tuberous nor foliage begonias. Surely it is time to simplify the schedules.

Pot Plants

Unlike the group classes it must be remembered that judges may, and often do, remove the pots from the staging for thorough examination.

Pot plants are not staged 'for effect', and therefore they sit unadorned on the staging, available for close scrutiny by the judges. The practice of covering the pots with black cloth should not be encouraged since it comes close to staging for effect, and in any case judges should be careful to scrutinize every aspect of the whole plant and that always means having to move it. It is therefore essential that the pots are clean, or as clean as you can get them.

Also note that plants in a multi-pot class will probably have been grown in pots of identical or near-identical size, though they may not be pots of the same colour or manufacture. To improve the overall look and give a degree of uniformity it is a good idea to take along a number of pots which are identical in size and colour (clean plastic ones are ideal), and to drop the plants and their pots into these containers. All yellowing, decayed or insect-bitten foliage must be removed, any rot must have been properly treated, and no disease or insect pest should be present.

Every plant should be properly 'dressed'. This means the stems should be securely fastened to the stakes, that no stake should appear above the foliage, and the blooms should be lifted with the aid of bloom supports so that they stare the judges in the face. The stakes and bloom supports should, however, not intrude on the overall appearance of the plant. With great care the bloom supports should be gently used to move flowers so that as many as possible are seen to the best advantage, spacing them out so that they do not obscure the view of any other bloom. It might be occasionally necessary to remove the odd leaf or two so that a particular bloom may be better seen, though this activity should be kept to the absolute minimum.

Having adjusted the flower supports so that the flowers can be seen to the best advantage, and checked that no leaves obscure a full view of the blooms, the plant is now turned so that its best aspect is that observed from the front. With multi-stemmed plants it is usual for two stems to be visible from the front, and occasionally this means that the flowers are collected into two groups, with a gap between. Efforts should be made to ease one or more blooms into this gap to achieve the appearance of one large head of bloom.

Although pot plants are not staged 'for effect' it is nevertheless sensible to arrange them in as pleasant a way as is possible. For example an exhibit of three pots may be staged in a row running from the front to the back of the staging. By standing the pots on wooden blocks the heights of the plants can be altered so that all are readily visible from the front. Alternatively they may be staged with two at the rear and one in front, again using blocks to raise the back two slightly. With pot plants there is no need to cover the pots, indeed the only justification for so doing is to make the exhibit more pleasing to the public after the judging.

In the case of pot plant classes involving restricted size pots, it is vital that the schedule is very carefully read and understood. If you are in any doubt then the show secretary should be contacted well in advance to clarify a problem. The current situation in England is that the pot size may not exceed a certain diameter, though this itself can pose problems since more and more pot manufacturers are using metric measurements for linear dimensions and volume. The growth habit of the plant is less debatable though frequently misunderstood. Only one main stem is allowed to develop, and from it no more than three side shoots. The only flowers which may be produced shall be on these four stems, and any other side shoots (wherever they grow) shall either be removed or remain, but never in flower.

Cut Blooms

Cut blooms of Tuberous, double begonias are displayed on bloom boards, which are made according to the following specifications based on a 9in (23cm) square per bloom.

For 1 bloom	9 × 9in (23 × 23cm)
For 3 blooms	9 × 27in (23 × 68.5cm)
For 6 blooms	18 × 27in (45 × 68.5cm)
For 12 blooms	36 × 27in (90 × 68.5cm)

Essentially the so-called bloom boards are wooden boxes with the external dimensions as above, with the rear-of-box height no greater than 9in (23cm), and the front no higher than 3in (7.5cm). The flat top surface of the box should carry circular holes at the centre of each 9in (23cm) square, large enough in which to place plastic beakers so that they will stand about 1in (2.5cm) proud of the board. The box should be painted matt black or covered with black material; many cut bloom experts choose black velvet.

The bloom boards for 12 cut blooms can be tiered if that style is preferred, and it is true that this makes for a more attractive presentation.

The beakers contain water or, alternatively, a mixture of one teaspoon of Milton, one of Alum, and one of sugar dissolved in 1gl (4.5l) of water. It is claimed that this maintains the freshness of the blooms for a longer period than does clean water. As an alternative the commercial product Chrysal may be used.

The cut blooms are carefully removed from their carrying box, and the bloom tube is removed. At no time should the face of the bloom be touched or this will mark the petals. The stems of the cut blooms are cut diagonally (to give the largest area of cut surface)

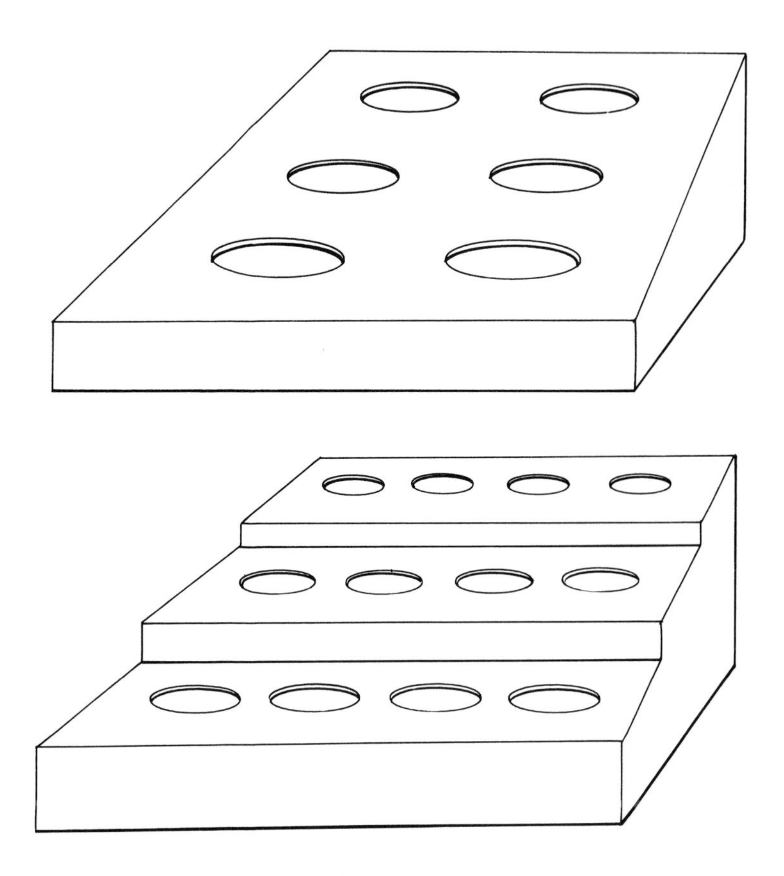

Two alternative types of bloom board for staging cut blooms. The tiered type is used only for twelve cut blooms. The boxes should be sprayed matt black, or in the case of the tiered type, covered in black velvet.

using a sharp knife, and when placed in the beaker the back petals should just rest on the rim of the container. The final height of the bloom may now be adjusted by adding more beakers so that the petals brush the surface of the boards. The positioning of the bloom in the beaker, coupled with the slope of the board, are so designed that the bloom faces the judge.

Taking into account the requirements of the schedule in respect of the number of varieties needed in the class, the objectives should be fresh, unmarked blooms, all of approximately equal diameter and depth, and all at their peak. Wherever possible try to avoid more than one bloom of any variety being on the same board since this provides the judges with an opportunity to compare the two, and one will always come out worst.

Also, too many unnamed seedlings on a board are a bad idea since the judges will be unaware of the potential of such begonias, and they will find it difficult to make a decision. From the visual viewpoint the stronger colours should be placed towards the rear of the board. When moving blooms around during staging to obtain the best visual effect, care should be taken to avoid water dripping on to the face of the board since this will wet the lower petals and detract from the perfect bloom.

As a final step ensure that all plants and blooms are correctly named, that you have the correct class entry card, and that the entry fully meets the requirements of the schedule.

JUDGING

Although one person's considered judgement will probably be slightly different from another's there are undoubtedly few issues on which most people will disagree.

At the present time most of the judging of begonias in Britain is 'appreciation judging'. It does not resort to giving points to blooms and plants unless it is otherwise impossible to differentiate between two or more exhibits and, in spite of what many people say, this is extremely rare.

Some years ago the National Begonia Society had a very elementary system of 'pointing' plants and blooms (Tuberous doubles), though it was very rarely used. As a consequence the pointing system was withdrawn. However, from the exhibitor's point of view some indication as to how a pointing method might be applied could help in assessing the quality of the blooms and plants. A different situation exists where the Non-tuberous begonias is concerned, as we shall see later.

Group Classes

Where group classes are concerned the judges are first looking at the general quality of the plants. Are they at their best? Do they each carry a reasonable number of blooms? Is there an eye-catching aspect to the selection of varieties? Does the overall display look balanced in terms of colour, are there any 'holes' in the display, is there a focal point in the exhibit, and does it sag instead of being mound-shaped? There is little doubt that where group exhibits are concerned it is the overall appearance that impresses judges far more than the quality of individual plants, though obviously individual quality will help the general appearance of the finished exhibit.

Pot Plants

In pot plant classes much more emphasis is placed on the quality of the separate plants which constitute the exhibit. First, the plant should have a good balance between foliage and bloom which means, amongst other factors, that the lower parts of the stems should not be bare. The foliage should be clean, healthy and unmarked, and serve as a backdrop to the flowers. Though it is not always possible the objective should be to have a considerable depth of flower, and in general that means there should be a number of side shoots carrying bloom. Each flowering stem should be carrying three recognizable blooms, one just past its best, one at its peak, and the third probably a very large bud two-thirds open.

All supports for the stems and blooms should be as unobtrusive as possible, and certainly should not rise above the foliage. The blooms should be close to the normally accepted size for the variety (where known), and loss in size should not be compensated for by the number of blooms. Multi-centred (or no centre) flowers will be penalized, as will blotched blooms, picotees and bicolours where the colours have run, and to a lesser extent plants that have suffered a small amount of travel damage.

Cut Blooms

Cut bloom classes are, in some ways, perhaps the most demanding type of begonia exhibit since all the judges' attention is focused on a relatively small number of flowers. Every small blemish seems to be highlighted, and there is virtually no way in which the exhibitor can cover up or hide the faults which he knows are present, even though the attempt is frequently made. There are certain aspects of cut bloom exhibits, however, which can be commented upon and which in a sense are the goals to which everyone strives.

First, where more than one bloom is called for they must be selected so that they are matched as closely as possible for size. It does not matter if you have a single bloom which is perfect and of enormous size, if it cannot be matched by the others in the class then it simply should not be used. Whilst size is important – and no bloom of a named variety should be shown unless it is at least of the dimensions expected of the cultivar – it is not necessarily the most important. The list of criteria runs as follows: the bloom should be fresh; have only one centre; be perfect in colour with a circular outline; have good depth with the correct spacing between petals; and have completely undamaged petals.

The question of bloom size is one which generates much heat but very little illumination when begonia enthusiasts get together. Certainly there are now varieties which are quite capable of giving huge blooms, though a degree of quality frequently has to be sacrificed on the altar of size. Some of the decrease in refinement can readily be seen, as with the appearance of small callouses (warts) between the petals. (In fact these are really undeveloped petals produced in quantity.) Other coarsening characteristics are not so easy to define but may be seen clearly, and include excessive veining in the petals, raggedness in the bloom centre, and a slight separation of the component colour pigments in blooms with pastel shades. It is much more satisfactory to obtain somewhat smaller blooms where these characteristics are not present and, for instance, a large, coarse bloom is certainly inferior to a smaller but refined flower.

As one becomes more experienced in growing plants for show, the inherent faults with certain varieties result in those plants being set aside in favour of others which do not have these problems. For example, the cultivar 'Fairylight' shows a considerable tendency for one petal to double back on itself (a characteristic of several other cultivars). This fault is more noticeable with the picotees than with self-coloured cultivars, such as 'Apricot Delight', because the changing direction of the contrasting coloured margin is clearly seen against the white or cream background. The variety 'Sceptre' has the characteristic of producing blooms with no recognizable centre, a fault also seen with the cultivar 'Margaret'. The variety 'Bonfire' is capable of producing very large heavy blooms, though many of them are multi-centred. 'Red Admiral', in the author's opinion a most attractive vibrant shade of red with slightly waved petals, is unfortunately at its best for only a short spell, making it hard to get its peak to coincide with the day of the show.

Obviously such issues will be overcome with experience, and as you talk to other growers about their successes and failures.

Judging Begonias by Pointing

In Britain the judging of Tuberous begonias is, in general, by 'appreciation' – the careful inspection of all the exhibits, with the poor and inferior being eliminated. The remainder are then more carefully scrutinized for faults and, in a rather ill-defined and unscientific way, are placed in relative order by the general agreement of the judges. After a number of years of judging I believe that, strangely enough, this approach does appear to work satisfactorily when judging Tuberous double begonias where every exhibitor is, by and large, using the same varieties. Perhaps, without realizing it the judges subconsciously apply a pointing system, in the mind, more often called 'experience'.

Where the Non-tuberous begonias are concerned, however, the position is quite different since the judges may well be called upon to make judgements between altogether disparate plants. How does one compare a Semperflorens with a Cane-stemmed begonia, or a Rex with a Hiemalis, and how does a judge assess a Superba against an Angel-wing Cane-stemmed begonia? Where Tuberous begonias are concerned no exhibit can be more than a few months old (in terms of growth) whereas, for example, one Rhizomatous plant could be one year old and in competition with another of perhaps three years' growth. With these Non-tuberous begonias. pointing could well make fair judging much more likely and its use could indeed be justified.

The pointing of begonias discussed below is not intended for judges but for those growers who, perhaps new to competition, have no guidance as to what might be expected of the plants and blooms on the show bench. The suggested points do not in any way reflect those of any society, and are merely the author's suggestions in an attempt to assist would-be exhibitors.

Tuberous Begonias

In the pointing system at one time adopted by the National Begonia Society (England & Wales), there was a vague procedure for rewarding good cultivation and recognizing faults, though the magnitude of the rewards and the relative penalties were never quantified, being left to the judges. The approach which follows appears to be complicated, but it really is not, and it should help the novice exhibitor to evaluate the quality of the plants and blooms being grown.

Pot Plants

A perfect pot plant would be awarded a total of 100 points from the following categories.

(a) Standard of cultivation – a well-balanced plant in terms of height and width with plenty of good-size blooms, each perfect. Healthy foliage.	20 points
(b) Quantity of bloom	15 points
(c) Quality of bloom	30 points
(d) Size of blooms	15 points
(e) Foliage	20 points

Each of these separate contributions could be made up in the following way:

(a) Standard of cultivation	
Shape of plant	10 points
Size of plant	5 points
Staking	2 points
Health of plant	3 points
	20 points
(b) Quantity of blooms	
At least 6 blooms per main stem	15 points
Between 4–6 blooms per main stem	13 points
Between 2–4 blooms per main stem	10 points
Less than 2 blooms per main stem	8 points
(c) Quality of blooms	
Freedom from faults	6 points
Bloom colour	6 points
Bloom shape	6 points
Travel damage	6 points
Freshness of blooms	6 points
	30 points
(d) Size of blooms	
All blooms of average size for variety	15 points
Most blooms of average size	13 points
Most less than average	10 points
(e) Foliage	
Colour of foliage	2 points
Quantity of foliage	4 points
No yellow foliage	4 points
No holes in foliage	4 points
Healthy foliage	6 points
	20 points

The individual scores in a, c and e will be reduced according to the presence of faults. For slight travel damage in c there might be a penalty, reducing the maximum 6 points to perhaps 5.

Cut Blooms

Taking a standard bloom size as 8in (20cm) diameter, a perfect bloom could be awarded 10 points as follows:

Single, undivided centre	2 points
Purity of colour	2 points
Bloom shape	2 points
Absence of faults	4 points
	10 points

These scores should be reduced by 1 point for a multi-centre, 0.5 for a shallow or an oval bloom, and 0.5 for each damaged petal(s), adventitious growths, colour run or blotching, and generally aged blooms.

Non-Tuberous Begonias

Assessing the relative merits of the Non-tuberous begonias can be considerably more difficult than for the Tuberous types, simply because of the heterogeneity of the various groups, the hybrids, and the species which make up these groups. Any acceptable system has to be kept simple, and the following is proposed for a perfect plant:

Culture	40 points
Foliage	30 points
Quantity of bloom	15 points
Difficulty of cultivation	15 points

In the case of Rex types the 15 points for bloom should be redistributed between foliage and culture; the quantity of bloom should also take into account the normal flowering season for the variety. Culture should include the maturity of the plant, in which instance a very young plant should incur a penalty of perhaps up to 10 points.

And finally I must reiterate that the above scoring system is a purely personal view, and is set out to help growers and not judges.

12 HYBRIDIZING

HISTORY

As might be expected after many decades of active hybridizing, the range of cultivars being grown today is very large indeed. This is certainly much truer of certain groups of begonias, such as the Tuberous section, where for many decades so much effort has been focused on the single objective of producing bigger and better large-flowered doubles.

These modern-day hybrids are so vastly different from the parents that many growers no longer have any real concept of what the original species looked like. Unfortunately much of the intensive breeding that has taken place has gone unrecorded, so continuing the process of crossing these cultivars is very much taking a leap in the dark, and may of course result in certain undesirable characteristics. The reasons why so many cultivars disappear (particularly in the Tuberous group) are not always easy to determine. In some instances it is simply that new varieties have been developed which are quite clearly improvements, but in other cases it appears that they have just gone out of fashion.

The situation is somewhat different with other groups of begonias. For example with the Cane-stemmed and the Rexes the registration process of the American Begonia Society means that, in many instances, the complete parentage of a registered hybrid is known. Of course this does not mean that every hybrid in this and other groups has been registered (indeed this is very far from the case), but it does mean that one can chose to breed from plants with known parentage.

Additionally, with these foliage begonias many of the original species exist and are widely grown, as are the very early generation hybrids, so that the amateur hybridist has great scope for experimentation. Since viable seed can be obtained by crossing almost any two begonias the possibilities are legion, but it must be remembered that, with the possible exceptions of the Tuberhybrida and Semperflorens, all the other types will produce seedlings which need to be cultivated under greenhouse conditions, and that means making available a lot of space.

When one looks at the current Tuberhybrida (large-flowered doubles) it is very difficult to visualize what else could possibly be done. It must also be said that the chances of an amateur achieving a startling breakthrough are very small compared with those of the commercial growers. The latter deal with tens of thousands of seedlings every year, compared with the handful which the amateur can produce. In spite of this many keen amateurs are producing some very good seedling begonias and, I am sure are secretly hoping that one day they will produce something sensational – a new colour break, a reverse picotee, or a perfect rose-form bloom with marvellous texture. The chances of this happening might be as good as winning a State lottery, but it happens!

For the amateur one of the difficulties is that they have only the stock named varieties to work with, and the parentage or breeding line is unknown, whereas the professional nurseries do keep unnamed varieties which are known to confer specific characteristics to many of their offspring. It is also quite likely that the amateur does not have any specific objective in mind when making a specific cross, and this too is a great pity.

In spite of what has been said above about the present state of the development in Tuberous doubles, there are one or two objectives which might be worth following in a more organized way. This might include white blooms with much improved petal texture, varieties (white and yellow) which do not bleed pink colouring through the dorsal petals, a really true yellow with larger blooms, a range of show-quality ruffled types, self-coloured and picotees, and the introduction of fragrance.

It has been said one should not 'work with Tuberhybrida, the Cheimantha or the Hiemalis field. The chances of producing something unique are rather dim . . .'. Though there is a good deal of truth in this observation, I cannot agree with it since it completely ignores the excitement of attempting a breakthrough.

At this stage a plea must be made to all amateur hybridists to record the cross A × B where A is the female (pod) parent and B the pollen parent, and second, to be ruthless about selecting individual seedlings for growing on. There has to be a distinct improvement in the progeny if it is to be worth keeping.

It should also be everyone's 'article of faith' never to use a plant which has obvious faults in hybridizing. For example in the Tuberhybrida group you should never breed from plants which are known to produce multi-centred blooms even occasionally, have dorsal petals which fold back, produce petals often folded, have weak flower stems, have a reluctance to throw side shoots, or are susceptible to mildew, and so on.

With these provisos in mind hybridization should be encouraged with the keeping of meticulous and constant records. Who can tell, perhaps an amateur enthusiast will one day produce a compact, Cane-stemmed begonia with angel-wing foliage and highly perfumed large panicles of golden yellow flowers the year round. One can but hope!

For successful hybridization you need viable pollen and a receptive female flower, both being available at the same time. This situation does not always apply naturally and, if not, then steps have to be taken to ensure that it happens by some other route. For those novice growers who are not too familiar at recognizing the sex of begonia blooms, the female flowers always have an ovary just behind the bloom, and which frequently has three wings.

LARGE-FLOWERED, TUBEROUS, DOUBLE BEGONIAS

The highly developed doubling of the male flower has meant the virtually complete disappearance of the pollen-bearing stamens and their conversion to petals. Very few of the named varieties produce pollen-bearing male flowers in the normal course of cultivation, and so it is necessary to take steps to force the production of pollen. The procedure normally followed involves taking a rooted cutting of the variety and growing it on in a 3in (7.5cm) pot (unstopped), and without feeding. Quite frequently the flowers produced in September will include males, with a high probability of carrying pollen. The presence of pollen can be verified by observing the stamens using a hand-held lens.

OTHER BEGONIAS, INCLUDING SPECIES

Here the problem is often not one of the pollen shortage, but rather that the two plants to be crossed are not in flower at the same time. Frequently this can be overcome by anticipating the situation and collecting the pollen from the male flower when it is fully open, and storing it in the refrigerator in a sealed container until the female flower of your choice is available. The pollen is carefully shaken out on to waxed paper and stored in a small, sealed, glass vial – most pollen will remain viable for a month or two if kept at about 40°F (4.5°C).

POLLINATION

This is the act of transferring the pollen to the pistil of the receptive female flower and ensuring that it adheres. Depending upon the type of begonia one is dealing with, this transference can be effected in one of two ways. First, a dry sable-hair brush (the type found in a child's painting set) is gently passed over the stamens of a pollen-carrying male flower and the yellow/orange grains will adhere to the bristles. This pollen-laden brush is then gently passed over the pistils of the female flower, and the transfer of pollen grains is observed again using a hand-held lens.

An alternative method for the smaller flowered begonias involves removing the male flower from the plant and cutting away the petals, leaving the stamens intact. Hold the stripped male flower by its pedicel and gently brush it over the pistils of the female bloom. Repeat two or three times, making the same cross with different female flowers. A small label should now be attached to the stem of the female bloom clearly setting out the crosses, together with the date. This process of pollen transfer is better carried out when the greenhouse conditions are those of a warm and not too humid (about 50 per cent) an atmosphere.

If the cross has been successful, within a few days the petals of the female flower will collapse and fall away and the ovary will begin to swell visibly. During the next two weeks the seed pod will continue to grow and the stem will turn brown and become dry. At this stage the seed pod may be removed and stored in a dry, warm place until it ripens or splits. Before splitting occurs the pod can be put on a sheet of white paper and kept in a glass, open-topped jar. When the pod has ripened or has split the seed may be removed and examined for viability. When viewed through a hand-held lens the viable seed is seen to be roughly spherical, whereas the non-viable seed is flat and elongated.

Separating the viable from the non-viable seed and the chaff is important since the latter two components tend to develop moulds when the seed is sown on a damp medium. The separation is accomplished by placing the total contents of the ripened pod on to a sheet of white paper and blowing gently across its surface. This will remove most of the chaff and non-viable seed. Further separation can be carried out by inclining the sheet of paper whilst gently tapping it with the fingers. The rounded viable seed will gently roll down the incline leaving the chaff behind. The fertile seed is now stored in a warm, dry place, either in small folded pieces of tissue or in small envelopes of waxed paper. For extended storage the seed, in its envelope or tissue, should be kept in an air-tight container and placed in the fridge at about 40°F (4.5°C).

In general the seed will remain quite viable for many months, though the actual length of time will depend upon the particular cross. My own experience with the seed from Tuberhybrida is that it has remained highly fertile for up to four years. Some of the seed from crossed species has remained viable for two years, though how general this is one cannot say.

Finally, the novice grower must remember that where begonias are concerned, all crosses involving hybrids will produce progeny different from the parents, as will crosses between different species, but self-crosses of species will yield seedlings all of which are identical to the parents.

13
PROPAGATION

In this chapter I am only going to examine the production or reproduction of plants identical to the parent. (The issue of seed production is better left to the chapter dealing with hybridization.)

To anyone who asks, 'Why are we propagating our begonias?' there are several answers. In certain circumstances we might be increasing the stock of specific varieties, perhaps for the purpose of showing cut blooms, necessitating a number of plants for each prospective show plant. Alternatively it might be to produce stock used as 'trade-offs' for varieties being obtained from colleagues. Another extremely good reason for propagating begonias, certainly the Tuberhybrida, is that they do die unexpectedly, and particularly in the dormant season, often without any obvious signs of disease or disorder. That being the case it is prudent to have backup tubers of each and every variety. But the real reason why we propagate plants is that it is an enjoyable, and indeed obsessive pastime. However, while it is very easy to take the cuttings it is far more time consuming to grow these small plants through the season, watering them as required. The lesson is therefore take only those cuttings which are necessary to satisfy a specific objective.

Before examining the propagation methods for the various types of begonia discussed in this book, a few general remarks would be pertinent. One of the factors distinguishing the begonias which grow from rhizomes (the Rexes and the Rhizomatous) from most other types if that the former are very readily propagated from leaf cuttings. These leaf cuttings might be whole leaf or simply small wedges, and the technique is reminiscent of the propagation of African violets. For the other types of begonia, propagation is normally from shoots or shoot tips, depending upon the particular type of begonia. Slowly however, as we shall see, this situation is changing though the reason is not always known. That which follows is the author's own experience, and then only with certain examples. It is not claimed that all the methods are universal, working for all cultivars, but that they have succeeded with those named. It is also quite clear from discussions with many colleagues that the rate of success with any particular method differs from one person to another, and that eventually everyone has to find their own preferred technique.

LARGE-FLOWERED TUBEROUS DOUBLES

The traditional method of propagation has been cuttings, though there is now little doubt that leaves can be rooted, and that they will produce a tuber which will start up the following year and produce a plant identical to the parent. It might very well be that the leaf which does behave in this way has special characteristics, having at the base of the stem an embryonic bud which cannot be seen by the eye.

I have had some success with this method with the cultivars 'Fred Martin', 'Gay Gordons' and 'Thingamujig', and it is perhaps significant that each of these cultivars is capable of producing many branched stems during growth. The success rate was about 20 per cent with these cultivars, but zero with many others.

The method involves removing the lower leaf of a normal cutting very carefully, and inserting the leaf stem into the cutting compost. Then place in the propagator at 70°F (21°C), keeping the foliage well sprayed with clean water.

The normal cuttings are either extra basal shoots, taken early in the growing season or later, after the plants have been stopped. Alternatively they could be stem cuttings or side shoots taken throughout the season. The basal cuttings appear to root very easily and, if taken early enough in the year, are quite capable of producing a flowering plant late in the season. However, allowing a cutting to flower is not good practice if you are looking for a reasonably sized tuber.

When the basal shoot is about 3in (7.5cm) tall it is removed as close to the tuber as possible using a sharp knife, or preferably a scalpel. Suitable scalpels and replacement blades (Swann-Morton Type 10A) can be purchased from the larger chemist shops. An examination of the base of the cutting will reveal one or more 'eyes', or embryonic buds, essential for the further development of the ultimate tuber. Normally these cuttings need no trimming and may be rooted as they are. The stem cuttings or side shoots grow in the leaf axil and are removed by making two cuts, one parallel to the main stem and the other parallel to the leaf stem. Once again a scalpel is the most useful tool for this purpose.

The two cuts are made so that the small 'eye' at the base of the side shoot remains undamaged and attached to the cutting. Any

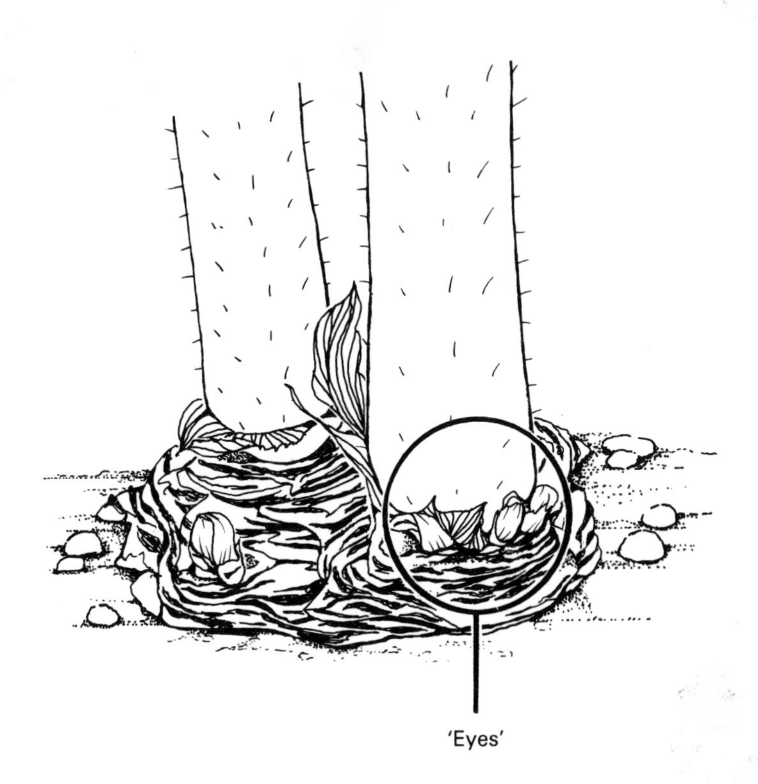

Basal cutting. A growth from the tuber can be used as a cutting if removed cleanly when about 3–4in (7.5–10cm) tall – then the cut should be made so as to include any 'eye' undamaged on the shoot.

flower buds on the cutting are removed. If the cutting is now examined it will often be found that along its length another leaf is carrying an 'eye' where it joins the stem of the cutting. By careful use of the scalpel this leaf can be removed along with its attached 'eye', thus providing a second cutting and, *very occasionally*, a third one may be found still further along the original side shoot. All of these cuttings may be dipped in rooting hormone and inserted in suitable compost, placed in a heated propagator at 70°F (21°C) and sprayed overhead regularly with clean water. The compost should also be kept moist, but not saturated, at all times.

Rooting should be well advanced in about four weeks when the cuttings can be taken out of the propagator and potted up into normal potting compost in 3in (7.5cm) pots. After about four weeks the growing points are pinched out, but the cuttings are kept

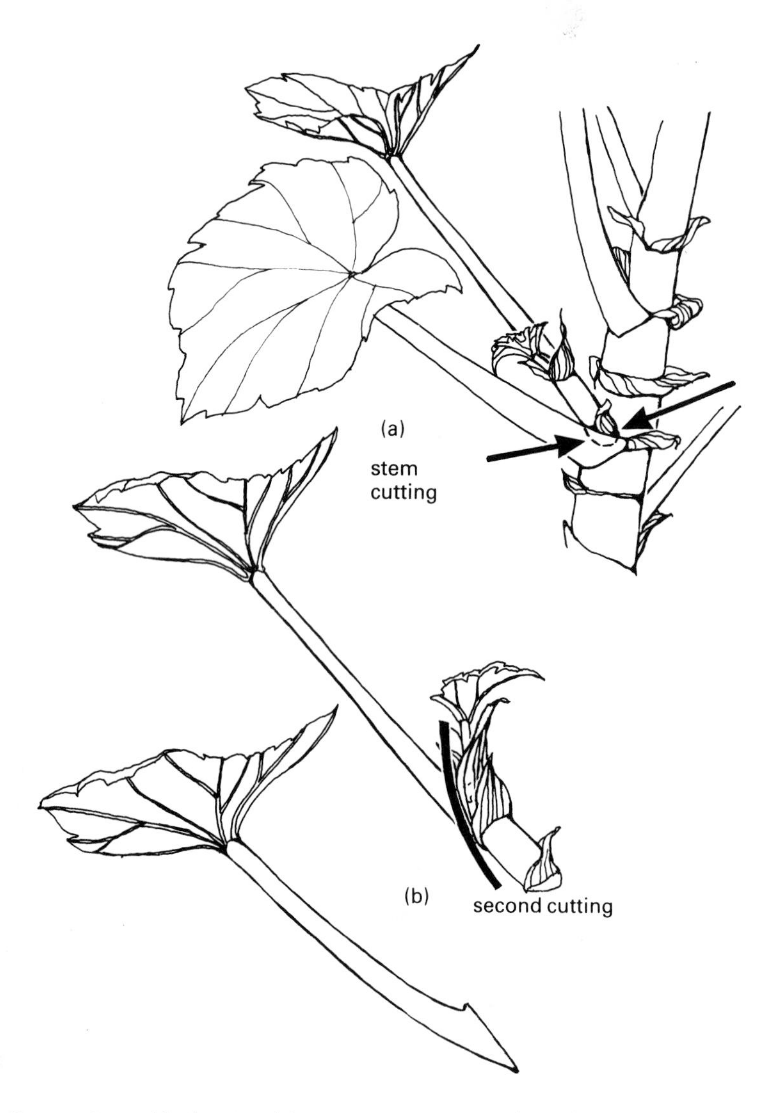

Stem cutting and leaf cutting: (a) a stem cutting is removed complete with undamaged eye; (b) a second (leaf) cutting can often be taken from either a stem or basal cutting.

moist and preferably in a cold frame until the possibility of frost arises when they are brought into warmer conditions.

As long as the cuttings are not too big my preferred container for rooting in the propagator are thin plastic trays, measuring 14 × 9in (35 × 23cm) subdivided into 40 small pots each measuring 1½ × 1½ × 2in (4 × 4 × 5cm) deep. When fully rooted the cutting, together with its plug of compost, lifts out and can be potted up in the usual way. Longer cuttings do not sit well in these containers and need their own 2½in (6.5cm) plastic pot.

When rooted, the cuttings can be removed from the small cellular pots complete with compost to avoid any root disturbance.

Cuttings in small pots do not need a propagator to root, and may be placed in plastic bags, inflated by breathing air into them. They are then tied firmly and hung in the apex of the greenhouse in such a way that they are out of direct sunlight at all times. With this method the plastic bags need to be large enough to prevent the leaves of the cutting coming in too great a contact with the plastic, otherwise water condensation will lead to rot.

Many of the problems associated with the failure of cuttings to root satisfactorily are due to the incidence of rot at the cut surface. Dipping the bottom ½in (13mm) of the cutting in a dilute solution of household bleach, or even Milton at 1 teaspoon per 1pt (0.5l) of water for about 20 seconds, followed by a spray of clean water, can help to reduce the tendency to rot.

An even simpler method involves placing the bottom ½in (13mm) of the stem of the cutting in clean water, and in a small bottle (a suitable container is one of the bloom tubes mentioned in Chapter 11). The bottle is placed out of direct sunlight, but where

Rooting in water. The cutting is inserted through the rubber cap so that the 'eye' is covered with about ½in (1cm) of water.

the light is good rooting will take about three weeks to commence. As soon as small roots appear the cutting should be potted up into the usual compost. It is a mistake to leave the cuttings too long believing that the bigger the roots the better the transfer to the compost.

Most growers will find here at least one method which will satisfy their needs for the propagation of their Tuberous begonias. However, if the success rate is still unacceptably low then perhaps it will be necessary to intall mist propagation. This can be expensive, though a handyman will find no great difficulty in making quite a satisfactory system at a relatively low cost. A supply of mains water is essential for this method. In principle mist propagation consists of a bed of sand heated to about 75°F (24°C) by a soil-warming cable fitted with thermostatic control, a fine misting nozzle, and a method of sensing the need for water.

Such a sensor can work on the principle of the changing electrical conductivity of a detector slowly drying out (an 'electronic leaf'), photo-electric cell, or a time switch. Whichever technique is used the sensor switches on a solenoid valve which allows the passage of water (under mains pressure) to the misting nozzle, thus periodically subjecting the cuttings to a very fine 'fog'.

Since the cuttings are kept very wet it is essential that the rooting compost used should have a very high air-filled porosity (as indicated in Chapter 15). Even if your success rate with any of the above methods has never exceeded about 20 per cent with mist it will rise quickly to figures in excess of 80 per cent. In very hard water areas there will sometimes be a problem when the misting nozzles become clogged with deposits of lime, but they can be easily and frequently cleaned.

As suggested, rooted cuttings can be grown on in a cold frame through the summer months, but a more convenient method is now being used by an increasing number of growers. The 3in (7.5cm) pots are buried up to the rim in the garden, protected from the direct sun by a suitable shade cloth canopy and watered by hosepipe every evening. The roots grow through the bottom of the pot forming a large root ball below, producing a most satisfactory tuber at the same time. Whether being grown on in the garden or in a frame, after about three to four weeks the growing points are pinched out. A dilute feed of a suitably balanced fertilizer is given to the young plants every three weeks to maintain vigorous growth.

Quite frequently, especially with the early rooted cuttings, a new growth will appear from the base which will produce flower buds.

These must be removed since no flowers should be allowed to develop. It is possible for the occasional strong cutting to produce quite a large single bloom, perhaps by September, but any tuber which has been formed will probably be extremely small and hardly worth the trouble. The only case where flowers should be allowed to develop occurs when attempting to produce pollen for crossing, and which is dealt with in Chapter 12, when discussing hybridizing. And finally, the pots are removed from the garden when the first light frosts of the autumn arrive.

PENDULA AND CASCADE BEGONIAS

These are always propagated from stem cuttings since basal cuttings are far too precious to sacrifice in this way. Since the main stems of this type of begonia are so thin the side shoots are even thinner, and cuttings are taken when they are quite small. Again it is essential that the 'eye' at the base of the side shoot remains undamaged on the cutting. The rooting methods are identical to those already discussed.

SEMPERFLORENS

It is quite unusual to propagate these begonias vegetatively since the majority of the modern hybrids are F1 hybrids and grown from seed. Occasionally, however, it becomes necessary to increase the stock of a particular variety, and this is done either by cuttings or division. If the parent plant is large enough, with perhaps upwards of 10 stems coming from the base, then take sharp knife and divide it into two pieces. This is the simplest and quickest means of propagation. Each piece can be potted up into fresh compost. Alternatively, a side shoot can be removed and rooted in a suitable compost. It is better to use a side shoot that already shows some evidence of branching since that characteristic will be passed on to the new plant. The double-flowered Semperflorens are always propagated in this manner.

HIEMALIS AND RIEGER BEGONIAS

Whereas the Hiemalis begonias are the result of crossing *B. socotrana* with Tuberous hybrids, the Hiemalis-like begonias have a slightly different background in that Rhizomatous types were included in the breeding. Not surprisingly, therefore, it is quite possible to propagate these begonias either by stem cuttings or by leaf cuttings (see later). A side shoot of about 3in (7.5cm) length, or a small leaf with its stem reduced to a length of 1in (2.5cm), will root very easily in an open peat/perlite compost at 70°F (21°C). If you have a substantial collection of Hiemalis-like begonias then it is wise to try out both propagating methods since some varieties respond to one method better than to the other. In general, the leaf propagation method appears to produce propagations which are prolific in producing basal growths.

CHEIMANTHA OR WINTER-FLOWERING BEGONIAS

This group of begonias directly results from crossing two Tuberous species, and has a semi-dormant period in summer (in the northern hemisphere). The group propagates very readily from stem cuttings taken from October to December, and rooted in an open compost at 70°F (21°C). The major problem with these cuttings is providing them with sufficient light at this time of the year. Cheimantha begonias may also be propagated by leaf cuttings, though this is more difficult.

The question of light values for cuttings in the autumn and winter months is quite important. For instance, in the case of the large-flowered, Tuberous, double begonias some of the best cutting material (basal shoots) is produced usually from August onwards, after the plants have been stopped. In order to produce sensibly sized tubers for the following year, it is necessary to grow the cuttings on through the winter months where the daylight hours are severely restricted to the point where growth all but ceases. This necessitates supplementing the daylength with additional lighting.

This is readily done by suspending a fluorescent tube about 12in (30cm) above the cuttings. A warm daylight tube, or a special Growlux horticultural version, would be sufficient to maintain growth through the winter. A twin tube fitting, some 2ft (60cm) long, will operate at a very low hourly cost and will satisfactorily illuminate an area 3 × 3ft (90 × 90cm). A time switch in the lighting circuit will enable the daylength to be controlled to 15 hours, which should be adequate.

OTHER TUBEROUS BEGONIAS (MULTIFLORA, NON-STOPS, ETC.)

All of these begonias may be propagated from cuttings, either basal or stem, though in practical terms it is the use to which they are put which tends to determine the method by which one increases stock. For example, the Non-stops and Clips are normally used as garden bedding plants, and in quantity. They are therefore propagated from seed which can be purchased from most of the larger seed merchants. On the other hand the Crispa marginata and Fimbriata types may be purchased very cheaply as tubers, and are thus rarely propagated. The Multiflora types are always propagated from cuttings since, to the author's knowledge, no seed is available.

CANE-STEMMED BEGONIAS

The normal method of propagating this type of begonia is by stem or tip cuttings. It is highly desirable, but not always possible, to take cuttings early in the spring to allow the maximum growth period before the onset of autumn and winter. If, however, it is necessary to take cuttings late in the year then a little warmth and artificial light can at least keep them alive through the winter, ready to commence growth in the spring.

The tip cutting is the top end of a growing stem and is taken by severing the stem just below a node (or leaf joint) so that there are preferably three nodes left on the part removed. The lower leaves are removed and the cutting is inserted into an open compost, consisting of equal volumes of a peat-based potting medium and perlite.

After thorough watering the cutting is placed in a propagator at 70°F (21°C) in good light, but out of direct sunlight. Daily misting with clean water will greatly help the rooting process. If, however, a complete stem is being removed (say in the act of pruning or grooming) then a number of cuttings may be taken. Each of these cuttings will have three nodes with an intact growth bud at each leaf joint. Again the lower leaves are removed and the cutting rooted as above.

It is also possible to root these tip and stem cuttings by immersing the bottom 1in (2.5cm) in clean water, and leaving them until tiny roots develop from the base of the stem. As soon as these roots are visible the cutting is then potted up into the compost/perlite mixture (as noted above).

With the Cane-stemmed begonias the length of the cutting will depend on how far apart are the nodes, and this can be anything from 4–10in (10–25cm) or more. Cuttings of the latter type will require support in the pot.

The cuttings taken should still have growth buds at the leaf joints, although with the miniature canes their flowering ability is such that it is difficult to find a piece of stem or tip with an unflowered bud. This is perhaps the major drawback to the propagation of miniatures.

Stem cutting propagation may also be used for other types of begonia, such as the shrubby types.

RHIZOMATOUS BEGONIAS

These methods also apply to the Rex begonias, being an example of the Rhizomatous type. The propagation methods are either by rhizome or leaf cuttings.

A rhizome is merely an enlarged stem and carries growth buds along its length. Either a complete rhizome, or part of it, is cut into small sections with each piece having a minimum of two buds. The cuts are made cleanly using a sharp scalpel which has been sterilized by dipping it into methylated spirit. I prefer to dust the cut ends with sulphur, though this is not absolutely necessary. The pieces of rhizome are then laid on the surface of the compost and just covered by sprinkling more compost on top. Again a suitable compost is the 50/50 peat compost/perlite mix.

The container is placed in the propagator at 70°F (21°C) and kept moist at all times. If the rhizome can be cut up so that each piece is left with a leaf attached this is quite an advantage, and rooting does seem to be somewhat quicker. The tips of rhizomes can also be used in this way. This method applies whether the rhizome is a creeping type or one that is erect.

Leaf cuttings may also be successfully used to propagate this type of begonia, and two methods are normally used. The first method is used for leaves that are up to about 2in (5cm) in size, and uses the whole leaf. The leaf is taken together with about 1in (2.5cm) of the petiole, and the petiole is inserted into the compost so that the blade of the leaf stands clear. In the second method, which is far more practical for the large- and medium-leaved varieties, the leaf is removed and cut into segments; each one of these segments includes a small area of the sinus, and therefore a small portion of a main vein.

Some growers like to sterilize this portion of leaf by dipping it into a dilute solution of domestic bleach, though it is questionable whether there is any value in this practice. The segments of leaf (wedges) are now inserted into the compost so that the lower ½in (13mm) is buried and the wedge stands vertically. As with all cuttings, rooting seems to be more successful if they are placed in a closed container, a propagator heated to 70°F (21°C). The compost must be kept moist at all times, but not wet.

An alternative to the wedge cuttings involves removing the sinus and petiole using a scalpel, and shaping the remainder of the leaf into the shape of a cone. The base of the cone is then inserted into the compost to a depth of about ½in (13mm). The removed sinus can also be rooted by inserting the petiole to about half its depth in the compost. Small plantlets will form at the main veins, four or five to a cone.

With the Rhizomatous begonias it takes at least four weeks for rooting to occur, though towards the end of the year it could take considerably longer. Once again the rooting medium should be quick-draining, mixing one volume of peat compost with one volume of perlite.

POTTING ON

The rooted cuttings of all the begonias described here are moved up into their own pots when rooting is well advanced. The medium should be a richer one of, say, 4 parts peat-based compost with 1 part perlite. From this point on they should then be grown on as normal plants.

Propagation by leaf sections may also work for a number of other types of begonia, for example for some Cane-stemmed and some shrubby species, including *B. glaziovii*, *B. listida*, and some of its hybrids.

TISSUE CULTURE (MICROPROPAGATION)

During the past decade or so a micropropagation method has been developed primarily for named, large-flowered, Tuberous, double begonias, and with some degree of success. Under sterile laboratory conditions a small section is excised from a small growth bud and

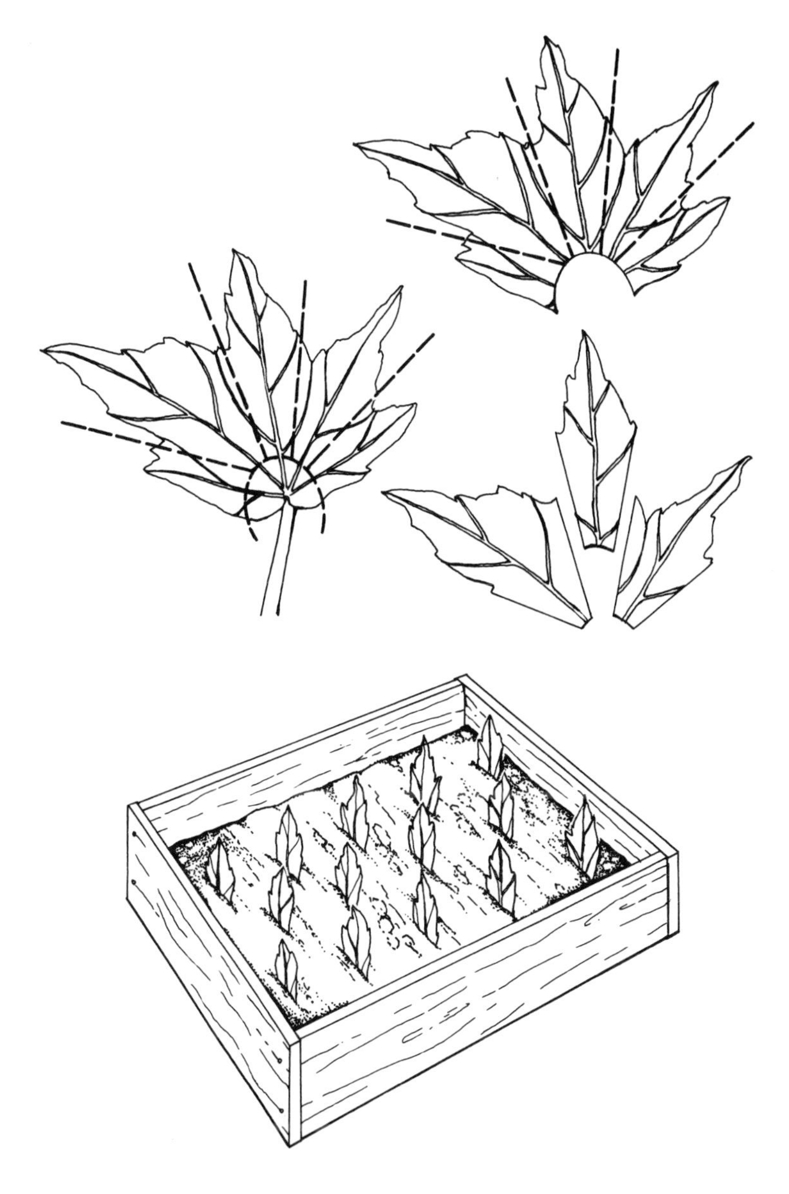

Wedge cuttings. The wedges are cut so that each contains a portion of a main vein – they are inserted into the compost so that about ¼–½in (0.5–1cm) is buried.

encouraged to multiply, using a suitable medium containing nutrients and growth hormones.

When the required degree of multiplication has been achieved, the tiny explants are coerced into forming roots by subtle changes in the composition of the growing medium. Eventually the plantlets are weaned from their laboratory conditions to be grown on as young plants in normal circumstances. This is usually the difficult phase since, at this stage, they are very susceptible to the presence of pathogens. However, with some good fortune and under the right conditions, this method can produce a few hundred plants identical to the parents in a few months.

If the method were indeed as simple as that, if all named varieties responded equally well to micropropagation, if every plantlet produced in this way was identical to its parent, then the problems of the commercial nurseries would be considerably lessened. Unfortunately in practice this is not the case and the major difficulty is an inconsistent ability to reproduce. Not all named varieties respond to the method, occasionally some plantlets will display a degree of mutation or, at the multiplication stage, all is suddenly, unexpectedly lost. Nevertheless, some of the commercial nurseries to an extent use this micropropagation method. One organization uses micropropagation to obtain a quick 'bulk up' of a new variety, and then propagates each of the plants obtained by normal techniques.

It is difficult to see what the value of micropropagation could be to the amateur grower, though it is true to say that amateur orchid growers now employ very similar techniques. If you are interested some very simple, but expensive, equipment is now available, and the growing medium can also be purchased fairly readily.

As far as can be ascertained no other type of begonia is yet being propagated in this way, though one cannot see why not. Presumably possible development along these lines is governed by the economics of the method.

14
PESTS AND DISEASES

Like all growing subjects, begonias are invaded by pests and attacked by diseases, but they are not prone to any particular problem. The best advice is prevention is always better than a cure, and this applies to insect and mite attack, to the onset of disease, and to problems associated with deficiencies in the essential nutrients.

It goes without saying that the provision of a good atmospheric environment, the purchasing of healthy stock, the use of a good growing medium and the correct attention to good hygiene will go a long way to ensuring a trouble-free life with begonias. Nevertheless unfortunately, problems do occur from time to time, and the purpose of this chapter is to suggest fruitful ways of tackling these difficulties. In the majority of cases problems arrive unannounced and have to be dealt with immediately, and this invariably involves the use of unpleasant chemicals.

It is of considerable importance that all horticultural chemicals are treated with the greatest respect both when they are being used and stored. They must be kept where children cannot find them; they must always be kept in their original, labelled containers; and any excess diluted materials should be disposed of immediately after use, followed by a thorough washing of the hands. It is also essential that before use the product label on the chemical should be carefully read, hopefully eliminating the possibility of mistakes.

Various acts and regulations have considerably reduced the range of chemicals available to the amateur gardener, and it is illegal for such growers to use or even purchase the chemicals intended solely for the professional. The range of chemicals approved for use by amateurs does not offer complete protection against the entire spectrum of possible disease and insect attack, such as begonia mite and vine weevil. Commercial packs of insecticides and fungicides are usually too large for the amateur's requirements and there is the temptation to break down such quantities into smaller packs for friends. Apart from the obvious danger of this practice, it is also strictly illegal. Nevertheless, very occasionally the only possible way of eradicating a pest which has managed to gain a strong foothold in the greenhouse is to resort to the use of more effective chemicals than those generally available. If the use of a restricted chemical intended for professional use only is necessary, then it must be used by a holder of a recognized certificate of competence issued by such bodies as the National Proficiency Test Council.

The other area, in Britain, which is perhaps more disconcerting is that part of the Control of Pesticide Regulations (1986) which restricts the use of a chemical to that specified by the government. One thinks, for example, of Benomyl which is specified as a fungicide but which is also believed to be effective against mites, including red spider.

With these provisos in mind we shall now consider the possible problems one might encounter in the cultivation of begonias.

PESTS

Aphids

This usually means green fly or plant louse which, in a normal season, is of little consequence in the cultivation of Tuberous begonias, but which does affect both the Cane-stemmed and Shrub-like types. Periodically however, we get a spring and summer following a very mild winter when aphids are quite a problem though their eradication is simple.

Spraying with insecticides containing permethrin, derris, or malathion will eliminate the pest and by repeating the spray at five-day intervals should prevent reinfestation. The systemic insecticides currently available are better avoided and, in truth, hardly necessary.

White fly – though not an aphid – can also attack certain begonias, especially Semperflorens. Here again a permethrin spray can be most effective. For both green and white fly the more environmentally friendly 'fatty acid' insecticidal soaps now readily available are most effective.

Earwigs

These pests are a particular problem during flowering time since they have an affection for flower buds. They burrow into the centre of a bud, gnawing away at the base of a flower petal. When the bud eventually opens it is then found to be a petal missing and the whole symmetry of the flower is destroyed. Since earwigs are a particular problem at bud-development time it is not possible to spray the plants. Instead you should fumigate the greenhouse, using a smoke cone containing gamma-HCH. The probability is that fumigation will be in late August/early September, and since at this time of the season there is often a risk of botrytis use a smoke cone also containing Tecnazene.

Tarsonemid Mite (Tarsonemus sps.)

If not controlled this pest can, in a bad season, decimate begonias in greenhouse pots. Unfortunately the pest is virtually invisible to the naked eye. It can attack plants very early in their growth destroying the growing tips and causing them to go 'blind'. It can, and does, attack more mature plants resulting in the undersides of the leaves becoming pitted with tiny brown spots; finally the leaves become brittle, turn brown, and fall off. It does not take long before all the whole foliage is affected, and at this stage there is little one can do for the plant.

Another sign of mite are stems (including leaf stems) being covered in a 'corky' deposit. In some years infestations can be widespread and almost impossible for the amateur to control. To reduce the possibility of an attack it is a good idea to spray the young plants with a dilute solution of common washing soda, or malathion. Greenhouse humidity should be kept as high as possible, at 80–90 per cent. If an attack gets out of hand and is spreading throughout the greenhouse then it might be necessary to seek professional help, requesting a spraying with an insecticide containing dicofol, (for example Kelthane or Childion). This is an organochlorine insecticide which is banned to amateurs and can only be used by certified users. When such an attack has occurred there is a possibility that the mite might overwinter at the base of embryonic buds, and a preventative spraying should be carried out immediately at the start of the following season.

In the hot, dry conditions in Australia, where attacks from tarsonemid mite are prevalent, the growers spray the plants with a suspension of sulphur, made by mixing the yellow or green powder with two or three drops of detergent, and diluting with water. Most growers in Britain experience a mild attack of mite on Tuberous begonias every year, and early treatment appears to eradicate it. In certain years, however, particularly when there is a very dry, warm period in April/May following a particularly mild winter, an attack of mite can become an infestation and eradication becomes difficult. The usual experience of most growers is that attacks of mite have ceased by the time June/July arrives.

Thrip (Heliothrips haemorrhoidalis)

Similar to the pest above, though easier to eradicate. Thrip is a minute insect which attacks the foliage in the early part of the season, scraping away the under surface of the leaves and leaving small pits. In time these pits rot and turn brown.

The major difference between a thrip attack and one from mite is that the former tends to attack the entire leaf, whereas the latter concentrates around the base of the main vein, at least in the early stages. Again, increasing the greenhouse atmospheric humidity will help to suppress thrip. Spraying with derris, or an insecticide containing permethrin, will help control this pest.

During the main part of the growing season it is unusual to suffer infestations of either thrip or mite, but flower thrip can be a nuisance when the buds are developing. The tiny insects invade the young buds, but when they begin to open they are found to be badly deformed. Since one cannot use sprays when buds are developing the form of control must involve smokes containing permethrin or gamma-HCH. Choose a warm evening when the air is fairly still, the greenhouse atmosphere is humid, and when the ventilators can be closed for a few hours.

The western flower thrip, which spread from America in 1986 is a potential severe threat to begonias, particularly since their life cycle includes a period within the compost. Regular spraying with malathion appears to offer the best protection.

Vine Weevil (Otiorrhynchus sulcatus)

A pest which, as growers of cyclamen, cinerarias and auriculas know only too well, is not at all peculiar to begonias. Certainly one expert horticulturist has described vine weevil, together with the wood louse, as 'deserving the pest of the decade award'.

The weevil is small at ¼–½in (6–13mm) long, and is an off-white grub with a brown or black head, appearing crescent-shaped. It is this grub which does all the damage, for the parent – a shiny, black beetle about ½in (13mm) long – is fairly innocuous, and its only claim to infamy is as the parent to the weevils. The beetles (almost all are female, the males are rare) lay their eggs (up to 1,000 produced asexually) during the summer in and around the roots of the growing begonias. The larvae hatch after about two weeks, whereupon the weevils burrow into the fleshy parts of the tubers and eat their fill for the next three months, during which time they can cause an incredible amount of damage. The weevils then pupate and the adult beetles emerge in autumn (under glass) and repeat the entire process. In the open the life cycle is out of sequence with that under glass, the adults emerging in spring. This means that there is a threat of vine weevil throughout the year, not just during the summer months.

Usually one is only conscious of their presence at the end of the season when the tubers are removed from their pots, revealing their tunnelling activities. If damage has occurred at the crown of the tuber it is highly unlikely it can be saved. If, however, the damage is only to the fleshy parts, then, make certain all weevils have been removed, cut away any rotten areas, and immerse the tuber in a solution of water and Benomyl, captan, or supercarb for about 20 minutes. The circular holes, or tunnels, in the tubers are a sure indication of the presence of vine weevil.

If attacks of vine weevil occur year after year then it is advisable to incorporate either gamma-HCH or bromophos into the compost before potting the plants. Once the plants are growing away strongly an occasional watering with gamma-HCH will help keep the pest at bay.

One of the old gardener's recipes for dealing with vine weevil, and one which many growers claim still works, involves incorporating some naphthalene into the bottom ½in (13mm) of compost, and a little more into the top ½in. It certainly adds a little extra flavour to the greenhouse atmosphere!

Vine weevil is the pest most likely to be experienced by growers of Tuberous begonias, and some amateurs seem to have considerable trouble with it. Perhaps it is as well to anticipate the problem and always incorporate insecticide into the compost. Speaking personally 1989 was the first year since around 1964 that my tubers had been attacked, so it is possible to avoid infestations.

Leaf Eelworm

Two types are known to infect begonias, root and leaf eelworm, of which the latter is the most likely to be encountered. Root eelworm causes swellings on the roots and, in the case of Tuberous begonias, can be recognized by the galls or swellings formed on the surface of the tuber. Leaf eelworm causes the areas between the leaf veins to go yellow, brown, and finally black and parchment-like. The infestation eventually spreads to the whole of the plant which ultimately dies.

The eelworm is a minute nematode, invisible to the eye, which moves around the plant in its fluid or sap. Leaf eelworm can spread from plant to plant quite quickly, particularly when a film of water provides a contact between the leaves of neighbouring plants.

When eelworm is suspected, the plant should be immediately isolated. At the present time there is no simple cure for eelworm available to the amateur grower, but that does not mean nothing can be done. One possible treatment involves hot water, a method which has been so successful in eradicating eelworm from chrysanthemums. The recommended treatment means immersing the dormant tubers in hot water for 15 minutes at 115°F (46°C), followed by 5 minutes in cold water.

Though I have never tried the following method, and therefore cannot make any claims for it, C. Chevalier in his book *Les Begonias* (Appendix IV) says that begonias attacked by Aphelencus olesistus (leaf eelworm) should be treated by immersing the *whole plant* in water at 122–125°F (49–51°C) for 5 minutes. It is important to note that leaf eelworm attacks most types of begonia, not just the ones which produce tubers.

Plants suffering from leaf eelworm should not be propagated from, until it is certain that the pest has been eradicated. Leaf eelworm should not be underestimated, and neither should the appearance of symptoms cause you to destroy plants before the presence of the nematode has been confirmed by a horticultural authority.

Sciarid Fly

This is also known as the fungus fly or the mushroom fly, and is a minute black fly which is found on the surface of peat-based composts. It is not a particularly harmful pest. However, its larvae can and do feed on the roots of plants, particularly where some rotting has occurred or where the nitrogen levels are high, for example when dried blood is used as a source of nitrogen.

The only insecticide which is effective against the sciarid fly is one based on the chemical dichlorvos, which is unavailable to the amateur. Dichlorvos is, however, the active ingredient in a number of solid insecticide formulations (for example vapona), and one or two of these strips hung in the greenhouse will effectively keep the population of sciarid fly at satisfactorily low levels.

Caterpillars

Not a very serious pest, though the level of infestation can vary from year to year. Usually they become a major problem only when the greenhouse is sited under trees and the source of infestation is outside the greenhouse. Frequently they are noticed only when small holes appear in the leaves and it is clear earwigs are not the problem. The best remedy involves picking them off and destroying them. For people who are averse to this method of control there is now a chemical treatment, bacteriospeine, which is most effective.

Today there is an increasing interest in the biological control of insects, so reducing our dependence on chemicals (in any event sooner or later most pests develop a resistance to the constant use of a particular chemical). Although several such treatments are currently available, for example parasitic wasps against white fly, predatory mites against red spider, and predatory midges for greenfly, the amateur usually wants an immediate solution which, of course, means chemicals.

Vine weevil is a particularly nasty pest which is effective throughout the summer. A product is now available, called Nemysis, which uses a nematode (otherwise harmless) to enter the vine weevil and kill it. Though not yet greatly used by amateurs it appears to be a valuable weapon against this pest. Whether amateur growers are going to be happy about the deliberate introduction of nematodes into their growing plants, no matter how harmless they are, is indeed another matter!

DISEASES

Bacterial Ring Spot

This is a bacterial infection which very rarely affects begonias, but because its implications are so serious it is worth mentioning. The symptoms are light-green rings on the leaves; these rings may be large or small and, as the leaf ages, the markings merge into one another. If such symptoms appear on a plant then it should immediately be separated from all others.

Unless it is a very special plant it is probably better to burn it, though only after having the infection confirmed,and the compost. Do not use this soil for propagation. If you wish to try and save the plant it should be sprayed with a copper-based fungicide. It is possible that repeated treatment with the fungicide might eradicate this problem.

Powdery Mildew

Begonias are affected by two distinct types of mildew (Oidium begoniae and Microsphaera begoniae) which differ in their response to fungicides. Superficially the two types are almost indistinguishable – both start as small specks of an ash-like deposit which, if left for a few days untreated, soon covers the whole plant with a white powdery coating. Mildew at this level soon debilitates the plant which then wilts and dies.

The conditions which give rise to mildew are not entirely understood. Certainly the spores are ever-present in the greenhouse and the atmosphere, and are always being carried on the wind. Even inside the home begonias, together with many other plants, can rapidly develop powdery mildew. Good air circulation helps to reduce the onset of an attack, as does a reasonably humid atmosphere when the temperature is high, for instance during the heat of the day. When, however, a warm day with high humidity is followed by a sharp drop in temperature and an even higher humidity, particularly if the ventilators are closed, the conditions for an attack are good.

Consequently you should try to achieve warm daytime temperatures with high humidity, and cool night temperatures and low humidity levels, coupled with good air circulation. On the other hand, if mildew appears then moving air will rapidly spread the infection throughout the greenhouse. Certain named varieties of Tuberous begonia are very susceptible to attacks of mildew – 'Tracy Lawton', 'Jean Blair', 'Majesty', 'Corona', etc. – as are a number of Non-tuberous types – Semperflorens, Riegers, Cane-stemmed begonias etc.

Of the two types of mildew discussed, the latter (and most common), cannot be eliminated by the normal fungicides, such as Benomyl. The approach most likely to be successful is a fungicide containing Dinocap as its active ingredient, or alternatively with triforine. Dinocap is not a systemic fungicide and therefore more than one application will be required. In general, powdery mildew is a disease of late summer, though on rare occasions it has been known to strike at the height of summer.

Stem Rot (Pythium sps. or Botrytis cinerea)

This is a wet, brown rot which affects the succulent stems of begonias (especially Tuberous begonias) and which, if left unattended, will cause complete collapse of the plant and the subsequent death of the tuber. In its later stages the brown rot becomes covered with a grey furry coating as a variety of other rots begin to affect the damaged area.

Stem rot is a bacterial infection which probably invades the plant through already damaged tissue, for instance by careless use of the watering-can or a too casual taking of stem cuttings. Whether such infections can arise within a healthy plant is not known, but we are certain that a plant which has become sappy through too much nitrogen feeding is particularly susceptible to stem rot. The incidence of stem rot is lowered when plenty of space exists between plants, and where the atmosphere is kept moving, perhaps by efficient circulating fans.

The treatment for stem rot involves cutting out the area of rot with a sharp knife. And this really does mean the entire area of rot which, if examined carefully, extends a little beyond the obvious region of brown flesh. After removing the infected tissue the healthy flesh is swabbed off with a dry cloth, and Benomyl is rubbed into the open wound. This may be mixed with an equal amount of yellow or green sulphur. All feeding is stopped and the amount of water being given to the plant is reduced considerably. Stem rot, which appears early in the season, can be quite disastrous if not spotted early, particularly if it is low down on the main stem since if unchecked it can spread into the tuber causing its untimely death. Later in the season, from September onwards, stem rot quite frequently appears, but in general the grower can treat the areas infected much more robustly, almost looking on the surgery as early or forced dormancy.

It must be again emphasized that the cultivation of begonias does not involve the grower in a constant war against pests and diseases. It is sufficient to be on one's guard so that neither disease nor insect attack gets the upper hand. At the time of writing there has been no substantiated report proving the presence of any virus detrimental to the health of begonias, as is true of orchids and chrysanthemums, etc.

Invariably when you have been growing begonias for any length of time you notice slight abnormalities in some of the leaves, for instance small areas where colour changes are obvious, small deformities in the odd leaf, etc. In most cases one does not know the cause of these effects, but they are undoubtedly not serious. They are unlikely to appear the next season, and usually they are restricted to very early growth.

Cultural problems, such as yellowing leaves, dropping foliage, and flowers falling, are usually the result of compost which is either too wet or too dry, or draughts, and experience will correct these mistakes. Even more infrequent are examples of deficiencies in certain essential elements which can cause foliage to change colour or plants to develop only slowly. Such problems are often related to inefficient mixing of composts, and occur with isolated plants rather than with the entire stock.

It is important to maintain a clean greenhouse in which fallen vegetable material is quickly removed, and where rotting plant debris can not provide rich breeding grounds for pathogenic bacteria. For example it is quite possible that begonia (tarsonemid) mite can overwinter in the protected environment of the greenhouse. If the tubers are thoroughly cleaned before going into winter store then the only sites for overwintering will be decaying vegetable matter in the greenhouse. It is therefore a good idea to empty the greenhouse in the autumn and to clean the inside of the structure thoroughly, including the benches, using a suitable disinfectant. Jeye's Fluid, though pungent, is very effective. If the smell offends then an alternative is available, namely Physan, a colourless, odourless liquid which is used for cleansing dairy equipment.

15
COMPOSTS

Begonias, like many other horticultural subjects, can be grown quite successfully in a variety of media including those based on loam, peat, composted sawdust, tree bark, coconut fibre, or even coal dust. For many years in Britain the preferred medium for the cultivation of begonias, and many other plants, was loam-based, and the most favoured formulations were those which were developed by the John Innes Horticultural Institution and designated J.I. composts.

These composts were based on a strict ratio of loam, peat and grit or sand, to which is added the correct amount of chalk and base fertilizer. Hence J.I. seed compost, and three potting composts – J.I. Nos 1–3 – the latter containing increasing amounts of base fertilizer. The one favoured amongst begonia growers was J.I. No 2. Having established standard formulations however, the more experienced growers were soon modifying this basic compost by adding such ill-defined materials as sheep or cow manure, or even composted farmyard manure, and replacing some of the peat with leaf mould. In a short time these additions led to various jealously guarded 'magic' formulations and individual 'recipes'. Indeed there were almost as many types of growing media as there were begonia growers! However, whilst it is possible to maintain the strict ratios of loam, peat and sand, it is difficult to define and impossible to maintain a consistent quality of loam, either from year to year, or from one district to another.

Loam is a complex material which, in the original John Innes (J.I.) formulation, refers to the humus-rich and fibrous product resulting from the stacking and composting of the top 4–5in (10–13cm) of old pastureland, including the turf. Today the term loam is almost synonymous with just about any type of topsoil which, whilst it might be of good quality, might equally be so poor that it contains toxic levels of poisonous, heavy metals or sulphur.

The J.I. composts can still be successfully used (and indeed up to two decades ago were the preferred growing media for all begonias), though they are a considerable challenge to the inexperienced grower. It makes sense, however, to have thorough chemical analyses carried out on the medium (or at least on the loam if making your own compost) before risking expensive plants in them.

PEAT-BASED COMPOSTS

For the above reasons, amongst others, it has become much more common to grow begonias in composts based upon peat and grit (or sand), and which were originally designated U.C. composts. As long as the grit has been washed well free of salts then both it and the peat are relatively inert materials of consistent quality. In terms of the limited growing period of the plants they act as a medium through which the necessary water, air and nutrients can be supplied to the plant. Some of these composts use sphagnum moss and sedge peats, and they may be purchased as commercial products or home-mixed.

As far as the commercially available composts are concerned there is not much evidence that any one brand will give discernably better results than another, but it is important that the compost purchased should be fairly fresh. If the bag of compost has been standing out of doors over winter and has been saturated with rain then its fertilizer content will have deteriorated considerably. After reassurance by the supplier as to the freshness of the compost, plants can be potted up in the knowledge that the nutrient levels will be satisfactory. Concerns over its physical suitability will be examined later.

Here we shall concentrate on home-made composts, so that we can be certain of the contents and their freshness. First, though, a number of principles have to be established. Peat composts contain essentially two important ingredients (apart from fertilizer), which are:

(a) *Peat* – preferably long-fibred, sphagnum moss peat. Sphagnum moss peat is an extremely good material for holding water, being capable of absorbing up to 15 times its own weight. It is also quite an acidic material (pH 3.7–4.00) which has to be corrected if the essential nutrients in the base fertilizer are to be freely available to the growing plants. This adjustment to pH 6.5 can be readily done by adding the correct amount of either ground chalk or dolomite limestone. Sedge peat is a less desirable form of peat for begonia cultivation.
(b) *Sand* this should be the sharp, gritty type of sand and not the reddish, and softer, builder's sand. The term 'sand' is also taken to

include grit – up to ⅛in (3mm) – in all cases well washed to remove any deleterious salts which may be present. For specific composts it may be advisable to replace part of the sand by other inert materials such as perlite (an expanded diatomaceous earth or volcanic rock), or vermiculite (an exfoliated micaceous mineral). It is important to remember that when replacing some of the grit with, for instance, perlite, the latter can absorb up to 3–4 times its own weight of water, unlike the former.

For plants to grow they must be supplied with both air and water, as well as nutrients. The nutrients normally enter the plant only through the root system, and then only in solution, which obviously requires the presence of water. The source of the nutrients is either the base fertilizer included in the compost, or it is the liquid feed. In the case of the base fertilizer, part of the available nitrogen is present in a form which necessitates it being broken down before being absorbed by the plant, a process which requires the presence of beneficial bacteria as well as oxygen. (In the special case of foliar feeding the nutrients enter the plants through the leaves.)

In addition air (strictly oxygen), which also enters via the root system, is required to carry out essential chemical reactions within the plant. If air is not available around the roots then they die, the plant becomes infected by pathogenic organisms, and it eventually dies. There are plants of course which can satisfy their oxygen requirements by absorbing it through their leaves, but these tend to be aquatic plants or at least plants which live in water.

The water which enters the plant via the root system circulates around the plant, is transpired through the leaves and must be replaced continuously through the roots. For uninterrupted growth it is therefore essential that the compost be formulated in such a way that these requirements, a good and continuous supply of air and water, are satisfied. In practice it is the relative amounts of peat and sand, together with the particle sizes, which largely control the air content of the final compost since the base fertilizer is used in such a small quantity.

As an approximate guide for good growth, a compost must contain an amount of air equal to at least 10 per cent of its own volume, and 20 per cent would be even better. This amount of air is usually known as the 'air-filled porosity'. If this porosity were much less than the 10–20 per cent figure, then it would be very easy to overwater the plant, depriving it of the essential oxygen that keeps the root system alive. The roots would rot and the whole plant deteriorate.

Overwatering is considered to be the one major factor responsible for the death of so many plants, and the poor health of countless more. The condition of overwatering can arise in one of two ways, or from a combination of both: the wrong compost mix; and, watering too frequently.

I shall begin by considering the former, using a simple example. Cut four strips of newspaper to the following dimensions 1 × 2in (2.5 × 5cm), 1 × 4in (2.5 × 10cm), 1 × 6in (2.5 × 15cm), and 3 × 6in (7.5 × 15cm), and dip each one to the same depth in water. The damp zone on the strips will be above the water-level and will be the same in each case, about ⅝in (15mm) above the surface. The water has risen due to capillary action and the extent of this rise does not depend either on the length or the width of the paper. In a similar way, you should now take a medium which contains exclusively peat and say ⅛in (3mm) grit, and consider the relative situations with a seed tray, depth 2½in (6.5cm), a 5in (13cm) diameter pot at a height of 4in (10cm), and an 8in (20cm) diameter pot at a height of 5½in (14cm).

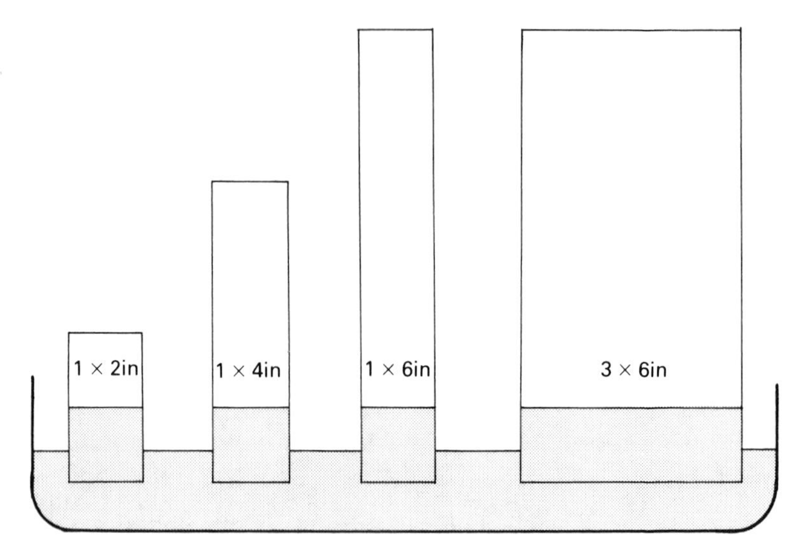

Capillary rise on webbing. The height of the wetted portion of paper does not depend on either the width or the length of the paper.

The individual containers are filled with the same medium and thoroughly watered. When draining has ceased each of the containers will contain the same depth of soggy compost at the bottom of the pot, again a result of capillary action. It therefore follows that since the individual heights of the containers are different, then the 8in (20cm) pot will contain more air than the 5in (13cm) pot which is, in turn, greater than the seed tray. In other words the air-filled porosity with a given medium is greatest in the tallest pot and can fall to low levels when the container is a shallow seed tray.

Indeed a compost formulated to give an air-filled porosity of say 15 per cent for raising seedlings would have an unacceptably high porosity if used in an 8in (20cm) pot, and would require very frequent watering to maintain plant growth. On the other hand a compost formulated for final potting could hold far too much water if used as a seed compost. As an example, one commercial compost formulated and supplied for potting was found to have an air-filled porosity of about 13 per cent in an 8in (20cm) pot, but this fell to 7.5 per cent when used in a 5in (13cm) pot, and still lower when used in a seed tray. Of course the latter, unacceptable figure could be increased by incorporating more grit, sand or perlite into the compost.

It follows that as you progress from seed or starting trays, through small pots to large ones, it is reasonable to suggest that there should a progressive change in the composition of the growing medium. In principle composts for trays and small pots should contain fine peat with adequate sand, whereas those for large pots should consist of coarser peat with added grit. It appears that commercial compost manufacturers do have different approaches to the formulation of potting media, one using fairly coarse peat alone, whereas the other uses fine peat with added sand.

An additional problem is encountered when taking into account the additional transpiration of water brought about by rising temperatures, falling atmospheric humidity, and the use of greenhouse fans. For example a rise in greenhouse temperature from 60–80°F (16–27°C) could result in up to a fourfold increase in the rate of water loss, and this would be further increased by a drop in atmospheric humidity which occurs as the temperature increases.

The important issue here is that whilst we concern ourselves about the degree of acidity or alkalinity of the compost (and it is correct that we should), it must be stressed that it is equally important that sufficient air and water is also available to the plant, at all times.

As with most problems one has to compromise between the ideal and the impractical. Since most begonias are grown in pots of 5–8in (13–20cm) diameter, the compost should be adjusted to give a porosity of nearly 20 per cent for the larger pot, falling to about 15 per cent in the smaller size. Seed composts need to be formulated separately since not only have the ingredients to be of small particle size, but the mix has to be far more open.

Air-filled porosities are relatively easily measured (*see* Appendix I), but it is probably more convenient to determine the rate at which a pot of compost drains from being full of water. This will give a very approximate guide as to the suitability of the compost for the pot size. A very simple method involves taking the relevant size pot and filling it to the normal level, compacting the compost as you would when potting a plant. The compost is then thoroughly watered and the compost allowed to settle. This is repeated a number of times until compaction is complete, and extra compost is added to give the original level.

A piece of polythene is cut to fit the bottom of the pot so that the compost cannot drain. The pot of compost is carefully and slowly lowered into a bucket of water until the level, rising up through the compost, just covers the surface of the medium. The piece of polythene is then held over the drainage holes. The pot is now taken out of the water, the pot surface is dried quickly by a helper, and the polythene is removed thus allowing the water to drain into a measuring jug. The pot is allowed to drain for about two minutes, and the volume of water is measured. If the drainage volumes are approximately equal to those in the following table the compost is probably satisfactory when it comes to supplying sufficient air to the roots. If the volumes are much greater then the frequency of watering will need to be increased, whereas if they are significantly lower the compost will need 'opening up' by increasing the aggregate content.

It must be stressed that the short drainage time of two minutes can only be used when the compost has a fairly high air-filled porosity and that the following figures are only an approximate guide to porosity.

This simple procedure can be used for any type of compost. Where home-made composts are concerned, the conversion of the peat/sand (grit) medium into a growing compost requires the addition of a suitable source of nutrients in the form of a base fertilizer (and there are quite a number of very suitable commercial products which can be used), together with a small amount of ground wood charcoal to keep the compost 'sweet'.

Though, as has been noted above, overwatering is a fairly common problem amongst amateur growers, it must be understood that a peat compost should not be allowed to become bone-dry either. Once completely dried out peat is extremely difficult to re-wet, becoming, as it does, almost water repellent. It is therefore a very

Drainage Rates for Various Pot Sizes

Diameter of Pot		*Volume of Drained Water*	
in.	**cm.**	**fluid oz.**	**ml.**
3	7.62	1.62	46
5	12.7	4.5	127
7	17.8	8.73	248
8	20.3	11.41	290
9	23.0	14.44	415

good precaution to treat the peat with a wetting agent before making up the compost. Non-ionic wetting agents can be obtained from horticultural suppliers at low cost, but avoid using domestic detergents for this purpose since they are normally completely unsatisfactory. This treatment is very simple, involving wetting the peat with a dilute solution of the wetting agent.

A good formulation, to start with, would be:

12gl (54.5l) sphagnum moss peat (fairly fine)
4gl (18l) g⅛in (3mm) grit, or 3gl (13l) grit and 1gl (4.5l) perlite
1 packet Potting Base
1 × 4in (10cm) pot of ground charcoal

In principle commercial base fertilizers do contain sufficient lime or ground chalk to correct the acidity of the peat and bring the pH to around 6.5. However, after thorough mixing, the compost should be submitted for analysis so that any deficiency in nutrients, etc., or too acid a medium, might be corrected before potting. The total nitrogen is normally of two types – that which is immediately available, and that which is longer term.

On the other hand, if you do not wish to use commercial-based fertilizers then the following formulation could be successfully used for 16gl (72l) of the above peat/grit mix:

10oz (283g) dolomite lime
10oz (283g) carbonate of lime (ground chalk)
4oz (113g) superphosphate of lime
1.5oz (42g) nitroform – slow release nitrogen
1oz (28g) trace element frit 253A
½oz (14g) nitrate of potash – rapid-action nitrogen
½oz (14g) sulphate of potash

One of the major problems encountered by amateurs who are preparing their own potting composts is that of the efficient mixing of the ingredients, particularly where the base fertilizer is concerned. It is of course possible to purchase rotary containers which it is claimed improve the homogeneity of the mix, though these are not exactly cheap. In practice one successful approach involves mixing the base fertilizer with the grit or sand. This is then added to the peat and thoroughly mixed, using the visual distribution of the grit as an indication of the completeness of the process.

For many years it was agreed that 'organic fertilizers' and peat-based composts were incompatible. The reasons given were that toxins built up in the compost through decomposition resulting, at best, in poor plant development and, at worst, the death of the plant. Recently, however, one organization has begun to market an 'organic peat compost'. A difficulty arises, however, in defining 'organic'. If one means from vegetable and animal origins then nitrogen and phosphorous could be supplied by finely ground hoof and horn meal, or from bone flour. A source of potassium is not so easily found unless the term 'organic' can also mean 'natural', in which case rock potash is just as natural as, say, bone-meal. At the present time very little is known about how such composts perform. If the grower suffers annual visits of vine weevil it is advantageous to incorporate gamma-HCH or bromophos into the compost at the mixing stage.

Peat Composts for Seed Sowing

The seed from most begonias can be successfully germinated on finely sieved vermiculite. However, since it is usual to transplant the seedlings into peat-based composts it appears that there is less of a setback when the seed sowing compost also contains peat. It is also usual practice to transplant the seedlings when they are still quite small, about ½in (2.5cm) high, and therefore it is unnecessary for the seed sowing mix to contain fertilizer. However, it is important that it is very free draining, and it should therefore contain a significant amount of very fine sharp sand or seed-grade perlite. From the discussion above it is clear that when maintaining an adequate air-filled porosity in shallow seed trays, coupled with a very fine compost, then it is essential to incorporate a significant quantity of aggregate. The peat should also be sieved to ensure a product which has small particle sizes. One must also remember that sphagnum moss peat has a low natural pH (high acidity) and, since no base fertilizer is being added, it is necessary to add finely ground limestone to restore the pH to 6–6.5.

For most uses a mixture containing equal parts, by volume, of finely sieved peat with seed-grade perlite or silver sand will prove quite satisfactory.

Whilst seed of most of the begonias discussed in this book will germinate in about three weeks, that from many others could take up to three months or more. For this reason, and the fact that for many weeks after germination begonia seedlings remain extremely small and highly susceptible to fungal attacks, it is essential that the sowing medium be sterile. Of course it is true that both of the above ingredients are themselves normally sterile, but it is foolish to take risks when it is so easy to give a 'pasteurizing' treatment before sowing. A truly sterile medium is one in which all organisms, beneficial as well as harmful, have been killed. It is only necessary to destroy the harmful variety, and this can be accomplished by heating the compost to a temperature of 140–176°F (59–79°C) for about 30 minutes. As with the pasteurization of certain foodstuffs the harmful organisms are effectively destroyed, and the process can be carried out in ordinary domestic cookers or microwave ovens. It is important that the whole of the compost being pasteurized must attain a temperature of no less than 140°F (59°C) and no greater than 176°F (79°C) and remain at that temperature for 30 minutes.

Peat Composts for Rooting Cuttings

Begonia cuttings, whether basal shoots, stem or leaf cuttings, are usually rooted either with or without mist. The two techniques are slightly different because when misting is used the compost is continually being wetted, and the very free drainage required means that the aggregate used to open up the compost should itself not hold water.

When misting is not used the medium need not be so free draining, and the aggregate used can be much more porous and water absorbent. With both types of medium there is an advantage in using a commercial, peat-based seed compost, to which an equal volume of aggregate is added – with misting ⅛in (3mm) grit, and without mist use perlite.

The use of peat is itself a controversial subject. On the one hand some people argue that the wetlands of Scotland and Somerset are being threatened by the removal of peat, and that the peat reserves are down to some 15 years at the present removal rate. On the other hand the Peat Producers Association, on introducing new codes of practice controlling the way that peat is harvested, assert that exploitation does not harm the wetlands.

In fact peat production for horticulture amounts to some 0.5 per cent of the peat available in Britain, and 1.0 per cent of the available peat in Ireland. Whatever the truth of the various arguments a search for alternatives to peat is underway. In principle the requirements are that they should be porous or able to retain large amounts of water, be available on a very large scale and constant in quality, be sterile, stable (that is should not decompose quickly), reasonably priced, and fairly neutral in pH.

Crushed pine bark is one possibility, but it does begin to decompose fairly quickly and needs treatment to remove tar acids. Composted sawdust is used widely in Australia, but this too poses environmental questions. More recently the use of coconut fibre has been claimed to be very successful, but this material could never meet the huge demands of the horticultural industry. Perhaps one of the most optimistic approaches is that of composting kitchen waste, sewage sludge and straw, to provide a sterile and readily available growing medium, though there might well be a degree of aesthetic prejudice against the use of such products. Some of these materials are now coming on to the market, and will need to be assessed in the near future.

LOAM-BASED COMPOSTS

As we have noted for many years the preferred, if not the only growing medium was based on good quality loam. However, the overall quality of the final product was dependant upon the source of the loam which was extremely variable. In an effort to standardize the quality and composition of loam-based composts the John Innes Horticultural Institute, in England, formulated a number of composts suitable for seed raising and the cultivation of pot plants, which were based on sterilized loams. The results were known as the J.I. seed or potting composts, and their introduction represented a considerable advance in the standardization of good quality growing media.

Many nurseries and garden centres still supply J.I. composts and will continue to do so for many years to come, though for many growers they have been superseded by the peat-based type. Most of the older begonia growers insisted that plants grown in the J.I.

composts had much tighter petals than those cultivated in the peat-based equivalents and that, as a consequence, their blooms lasted much longer. Whether this is true one cannot say, but it is interesting to note that today, after growing in the peat types for many years, one no longer hears this view expressed. There is little doubt that, as regards convenience, most growers now use the peat type of compost but for the sake of completeness, and for the benefit of those readers who might wish to cultivate their begonias in loam-based media, their formulation will be briefly considered.

If you are proposing to purchase a J.I. compost it is advisable to resort to a method of growing which requires two separate potting stages – for the first potting the J.I. No 2 compost is used, and No 3 for the second and final potting. If the reader prefers to make up his own compost the materials required and suitable formulations, are as follows.

Loam

This is the main ingredient which supplies the clay and the humus, so invaluable for plant growth. A medium loam is best and contains just enough clay to be slightly greasy when wet. It should have a pH of about 6.5–5.5, and a humus content of 2–7 per cent, which is usually assured by using turf loam. (Turves cut when the grass is quite thick and stacked whilst wet is usable in about six months.) If the pH is lower than 6.0 it must be brought up to 6.3 by the addition of chalk before use. The loam should be sterilized before use by heat, or by the application of suitable chemicals, and then passed through a sieve to remove stones and large clumps.

Peat and/or leaf mould

This is the source of humus and, of the two sources, peat is preferable. Leaf mould is very variable, often containing weed seeds and worms, and the quality will depend on both the age and the type of leaves from which it comes. Peat is a much more consistent material, it holds considerable amounts of water, is initially sterile, and is useful in helping to aerate the final compost. For use in composts the preferred peat is the long-fibred type rather than the powdery, dusty materials sometimes sold. Both the peat and the loam should be moist before mixing.

Sand

The sand used in seed and potting composts should be the very sharp, gritty types since they are present to provide good drainage. They should be washed free of clay and lime, as well as any organic matter. The particle size should grade from fine right up to the coarse particles of ⅛in (3mm) in size. The smooth, soft, red builder's sand is totally unsatisfactory. For seed composts the finer grades of sharp sand are better for ensuring good germination.

The J.I. composts are made by mixing together these three ingredients in the correct proportions, and then adding the required fertilizer. The proportions are as follows:

Seed compost: 2 parts by volume of medium loam
1 part by volume peat (or leaf-mould)
1 part by volume sand

Potting compost: 7 parts by volume medium loam
3 parts by volume peat
2 parts by volume coarse sand

This mix now has to be fertilized, which can be done in two ways – use a commercial J.I. base fertilizer, or add an equivalent home-made one in the following proportions:

To 8gl (36l) of either of the above mixes one adds:

Seed compost: superphosphate of lime 1.5oz (42g)
Ground chalk ¾oz (21g)

Potting compost: J.I. base 4oz (113g)
Ground chalk ¾oz (21g)

And the J.I. base is made up from:
Hoof and horn 2 parts
Superphosphate of lime 2 parts
Sulphate of potash 1 part

The J.I. potting compost, as made according to the proportions above, is known as J.I. No 1, whilst Nos 2 & 3 contain twice and three times the amount of J.I. base respectively. The procedure for mixing is also quite important if a consistent compost is to be obtained, and here the accepted practice is to mix the fertilizer with the sand before spreading over the loam and peat mix. After thorough mixing the compost is allowed to stand for a few days before using.

Of course, having been given a good, consistent, quality formulation, growers immediately modify it for their own individual likes and dislikes, for instance incorporating natural manures. In fact farmyard manure is not very rich in plant foods, though it is valuable in conferring good moisture holding properties and humus to the compost. On average, manure contains about 0.5 per cent nitrogen, 0.25 per cent phosphoric acid, and 0.5 per cent potash, though after standing for some time these figures will increase slightly. Cow manure is very similar in composition, but both types will vary depending on the method of animal feeding. One possible compost formula using manure is:

Medium loam	4 parts by volume
Leaf-mould	1 part by volume
Peat	1 part by volume
Sheep manure	1 part by volume
Grit	1 part by volume

While other very successful growers are equally certain that the natural product should be cow manure, everyone agrees that whatever kind of manure is being used, it should have been well rotted before use. Whether these many 'personalized' J.I. composts have any real value, above and beyond the standard types, it is quite impossible to say, but they certainly give the grower the feeling of being a little different from his/her colleagues, and that at least must have some therapeutic value!

We must not get the idea that the choice of compost is a simple one, between the loam-based and peat-based types. There are some extremely successful showmen who prefer to use a compost which is a 50/50 mixture of the two types. It is not easy to ascertain why they should do so, though there is one advantage against the 100 per cent peat-based types, and that is the plants are physically much more stable when the pot contains any loam-based compost. On the other hand such stability can be obtained even with peat-based media simply by putting coarse gravel into the pot before the compost.

Since loam, particularly if it is of good quality, is much richer in plant food than is peat, it is clear that the feeding requirements of plants grown in the J.I. type of compost will differ from those cultivated in the peat-based ones. Certainly there is no need to liquid feed plants grown in J.I. composts for at least 12 weeks after potting.

Many amateur growers now find that growing in J.I. type composts extremely difficult, mainly on account of the problems associated with watering, and usually the fault is excessive overwatering. The J.I. mix is much less open than the peat-based formulations, and with a considerably lower air-filled porosity. This usually means that plants grown in the loam composts need to be 'potted on' at least once to prevent the death of the roots, a practice which is unnecessary with peat composts.

APPENDICES

I AIR-FILLED POROSITY

As we have noted in Chapter 15, the air-filled porosity of a compost depends on the physical make up of the medium, and the depth of the medium. To grow begonias well it is important that this porosity should be from 15–20 per cent, thus ensuring that adequate air (or oxygen) is available to satisfy the needs of the growing plant. The air-filled porosity of a compost will depend upon its depth, being higher in the tallest pot and lowest in the shallower pot. In general the most frequently used pot sizes for begonia growing are the 5in (12.5cm) and the 7in (17.5cm) diameter types. The former has an internal height of 3¾in (9.5cm) and the latter of 4¾in (12cm).

To make the necessary measurements a suitable container is taken and the two heights – 3¾in (9.5cm) and 4¾in (12cm) – are marked on the inside using a waterproof label pen. A useful container for this purpose is one of the cylindrical tins used for the sale of ground coffee, and often supplied complete with a polythene lid. They usually measure 3¾in (9.5cm) in diameter, being 6in (15cm)–7in (18cm) tall. Six holes with a diameter of ½in (13mm) are drilled through the base, and the polythene lid is cut so that it covers all the holes.

Compost in its normal damp state is now poured into the container until the level is up to either of the internal marks. The container is now lowered into a bucket of water so that the liquid rises through the compost, wetting it thoroughly. The container is removed from the bucket and the water allowed to drain – this is repeated two or three times, and any compacting of the compost level is made by adding fresh material up to the mark. Finally the container is lowered into the bucket and positioned so that the compost surface is *just* covered with liquid. The polythene disc is slid over the holes and held using both hands so that no water escapes from the tin.

The container is now removed from the bucket and a helper quickly dries the outside surface. Whilst holding the container over a plastic funnel, which in turn, stands in a measuring jug, the plastic

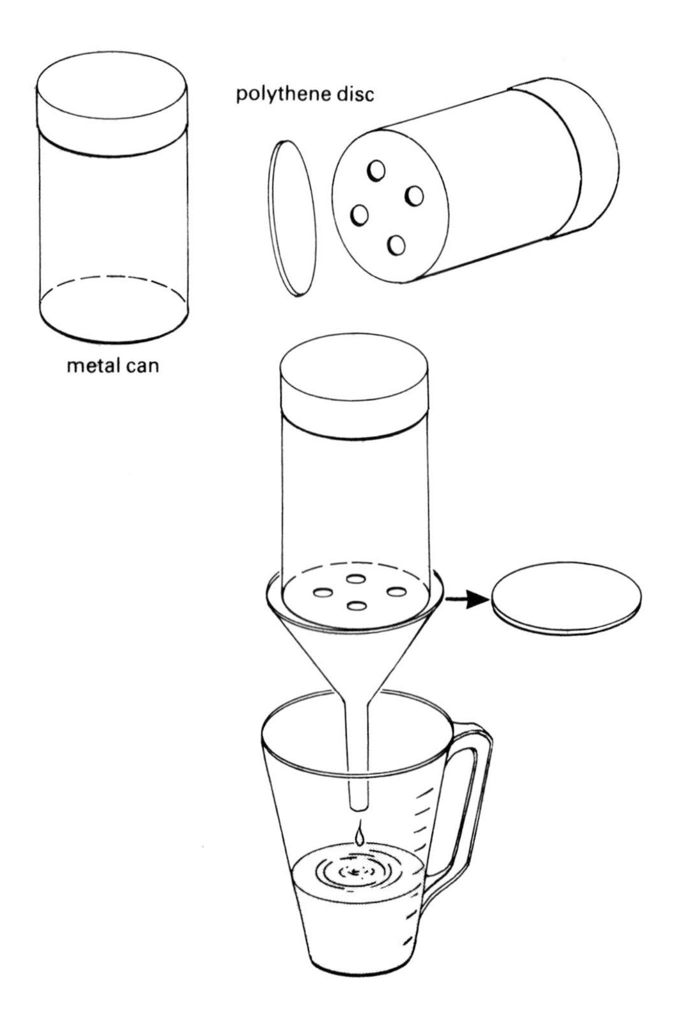

Measuring air porosity. The air porosity is found by measuring the amount of water which drains from a completely saturated compost (and which is replaced by air) during a short period of time.

disc is quickly removed thus allowing the water to drain into the vessel. Draining is allowed to continue for two minutes (the open compost required is very quick draining) and the volume of water drained is measured.

The air-filled porosity is then calculated as follows:

Volume of compost taken –

$$\frac{22 \times d(cm) \times d(cm) \times \text{height of compost (cm)}}{[7 \times 4]}$$

For example, if the measuring container had a diameter of 3¾in (9.7cm) and we were considering a 7in (18cm) pot with a height of 4¾in (12cm), then the volume of compost would be:

$$\frac{22 \times 9.7 \times 9.7 \times 12.00}{7 \times 4} = 887.13 \text{ cubic cms}$$

If 168.5 cubic cms of water had drained, then the air-filled porosity would be:

$$\frac{168.5}{887.13} \times 100 = 18.99 \text{ per cent.}$$

II ORGANIZATIONS INVOLVED WITH BEGONIAS

United Kingdom

National Begonia Society (England & Wales) Dr E. Catterall, The Secretary, 7 Springwood Close, Thurgoland, Sheffield S30 7AB.

The north west T. Tasker, 6 Sandheys Drive, Churchtown, Southport PR9 9PQ.

The south coast D. Coates, 126 West Street, Portchester, Hampshire PO16 9XE.

Yorkshire & Humberside J. Rhodes, 7 Tew Street, Denby Dale Road, Wakefield WF2 8DR.

East Midlands S. Greenwood, 41 Alexander Road, Farnsfield, Newark NG22 8LH.

Central region J. Robertson, 20 Monks Kirby Road, Walmley, Sutton Coldfield B76 8UN.

East Anglia D.R. Staines, 7 Mead Close, Walton, Peterborough PE4 6BS.

Scottish Begonia Society Mr G. Thompson, The Secretary, 24 Third Avenue, Stepps, Glasgow G33, Scotland.

The East of Scotland Begonia Society Matt Stobbs, The Secretary, 17 Lomond Crescent, Dunfermline, Fife, Scotland.

South-West of Scotland Begonia Society John Orr, The Secretary, 11 Nithsdale Avenue, New Cumnock, Ayrshire, Scotland.

United States of America

American Begonia Society Mr John Ingles Jr., The Membership Secretary, 157 Monument, Rio Dell, CA 95562–1617, USA.

Australia

Australian Begonia Society Inc. P.O. Box. 386, Woodville, S.A. 5011, Australia.

New South Wales Begonia Society Major P.G. Sharp, The Secretary, 20 Blue Gum Crescent, Blaxland, NSW, Australia 2774.

Victoria Begonia Society Inc. P.D. Wright, The Secretary, 'Maplewood', 74 Railway Place, Macedon, Victoria 3440, Australia.

Begonia Society of Western Australia Inc. S. Silvester, The Secretary, 34 Waterton Way, Cooloongup, WA 6168, Australia.

Queensland Begonia Society Peter Henderson, The Secretary, 79 Chuter Street, Staford North 4053, Brisbane, Queensland.

France

Association Française des Amateurs de Begonias Mme Annie Dananchcr, 11 Rue Myrha, 75018 Paris, France.

Japan

Japanese Begonia Society Mr Akira Tanaka, The President, 12–4–318 Sengen-Cho, 3 Chome, Higashikurume, Tokyo 203, Japan.

Canada

British Columbia Fuchsia and Begonia Society Lorna Herchenson, North Vancouver, B.C. V7H 1L2, Canada.

Belgium

Société Belge du Begonia Piron Gilles, The President, Chemin de Lancre 4, B-4970 Coo, Belgium.

III SUPPLIERS OF PLANTS, SEEDS AND ACCESSORIES

The following is a listing of Begonia plants, seeds and materials referred to in the text, as known to the author at the time of writing. In the case of the amateur raisers of Tuberous begonias, it is known only that the varieties described in the text are quite outstanding in one respect or another.

Suppliers of Large-Flowered, Tuberous, and Cascades

Blackmore & Langdon Ltd., Pensford, Nr. Bristol BS18 4JL, England. Mail order.

Parkers Dutch Bulbs Ltd., Chester Road, Old Trafford, Manchester M16 9HL, England. Mail order suppliers.

R. White & Son, Park Mains Nursery, Erskine, Renfrewshire, Scotland. Mail order.

Willsmore Begonia Farm, Blockers Road, Myponga, South Australia 5202, Australia. They export begonias world wide.

Antonelli Bros., 2545 Capitola Road, Santa Cruz, California 95060, USA.

White Flower Farm, Litchfield, Connecticut 067591, USA. Blackmore & Langdon named tubers sold.

Hiemalis and Rieger Begonias

P. Van Zelst, Barberry Nursery, Knaresborough, North Yorkshire, HG5 9EL, England. Sales to commercial outlets.

Nielsen Plants Ltd., Danecroft Nurseries, Hellingly, Sussex BN27 7EU, England. Sales to commercial outlets.

Bridgemere Nurseries, Bridgemere, Nr. Nantwich, Cheshire CW5 7QR, England. Sales to public and mail order.

Mikkelsens Inc., Box 1536, Ashtabula, Ohio 44004, USA. Sales to commerical outlets.

Multiflora Begonias, Non-stops, Clips, etc.

B. and H.M. Baker, Bourne Brook Nurseries, Greenstead Green, Halstead, Essex CO9 1RJ, England. Some Multiflora types.

Mr. Fothergill's Seeds Ltd., Kentford, Newmarket, Suffolk CB8 7QB, England.

Parkers Dutch Bulbs Ltd., Chester Road, Old Trafford, Manchester M16 9HL, England.

Samuel Dobie & Son Ltd., Broomhill Way, Torquay TQ2 7QW, England.

Suttons Seeds Ltd., Hele Road, Torquay TQ2 2QJ, England

Thompson & Morgan, London Road, Ipswich, Suffolk IP2 0BA, England.

Wallace and Barr Ltd., The Nurseries, Marden, Kent TN12 9BP, England. Marmorata tubers.

Semperflorens Begonias

All the seedsmen in the previous section, and . . .

Logee's Greenhouses, Dept. B, 55 North Street, Danielson, Connecticut 06239, USA.

Miscellaneous Begonias

Horticulture Ghislaine, Barrere, Les 4 Coins, Beaumont sur Leze, 31190 Autorive, France.

Daniel Benefice, 77, rue Jean Jaures, 26800 Portes les Valence, France.

Le Jardin Truffaut de la Ville du Bois, 91620 Ville du Bois, France.

A. Maurieres, Domaine Horticole de la Bellongue, 09800 Orgibet, France.

Les Serres de la Bellongue, Jean Paul Pelegry, 559 Route de Toulouse, 33140 Villenave d'Orgnon, France.

Bloom Tubes

Deathridge A.J. Smithfield Market, Pershore Street, Birmingham B5 6UN, England.

Flower Arrangers Shop, 11 Union Street, Stratford-on-Avon, Warwickshire CV37 6QT, England.
For the large-flowered, Tuberous; double begonias a diameter of at least ¾in (20mm) is required.

H.G. Hees, Orchid Supplies, 99a Kiln Ride, Wokingham, Berkshire RG11 3PD, England.

Greenhouse Shading

Barry Bryan Growers, Supplies Ltd., 10 Bonds Lane, Banks, Southport, Lancashire, England.
Spun polypropylene sold in different grades.

L.B.S. Polythene, Cottontree, Nr. Colne, Lancashire BB8 7BW, England.
High-density polythene knitted shade net 40, 50 and 70 per cent shade value.

Prylorn Ltd., Elmhirst Yard, 89 High Street, Chatteris, Cambridgeshire PE16 6NP, England.
Suppliers of the aluminium foil shading of Scandinavian origin.

Equipment for Handling Tissue Cultures

Safetech, Enterprise House, Plessey Technological Park, Limerick, Ireland.
Manufacturers of Cleansphere CA100.

Suppliers of Heated Blanket for Propagation

Prylorn Ltd., Elmhirst Yard, 89 High Street, Chatteris, Cambridgeshire PE16 6NP, England.

IV BIBLIOGRAPHY

Catterall, E., *Growing Begonias* (Croom Helm, 1984). Mainly Tuberous begonias. Horticultural.

Chevalier, C., *Les Begonias*; English translation, A.C. Graham (A.B.S., 1975). Deals with all species and hybrids. Botanical and horticultural.

Haegman, J. (J. Cramer 1979) *Tuberous Begonias* Tuberous begonias of all types. Botanical and horticultural.

Langdon, B., *The Tuberous Begonia* (Cassell, 1969). Large, double, Tuberous begonias. Horticultural.

Langdon, B., *Begonias* (Cassell, 1989). Large, double, Tuberous begonias. Horticultural.

Smith, L.B., Golding, J., Wasshausen, D.C. and Kareganncs, C.E., *Begoniaceae* (Smithsonian Institution Press, 1986). An annotated list of species. Botanical.

Thompson, M.L. and Thompson, E.J., *Begonias* (Times Books, 1981). Deals with the whole range of begonias. Botanical and horticultural.

Wall, B., *Begonias* (Cassell, 1988). A wide range of horticultural begonias.

INDEX